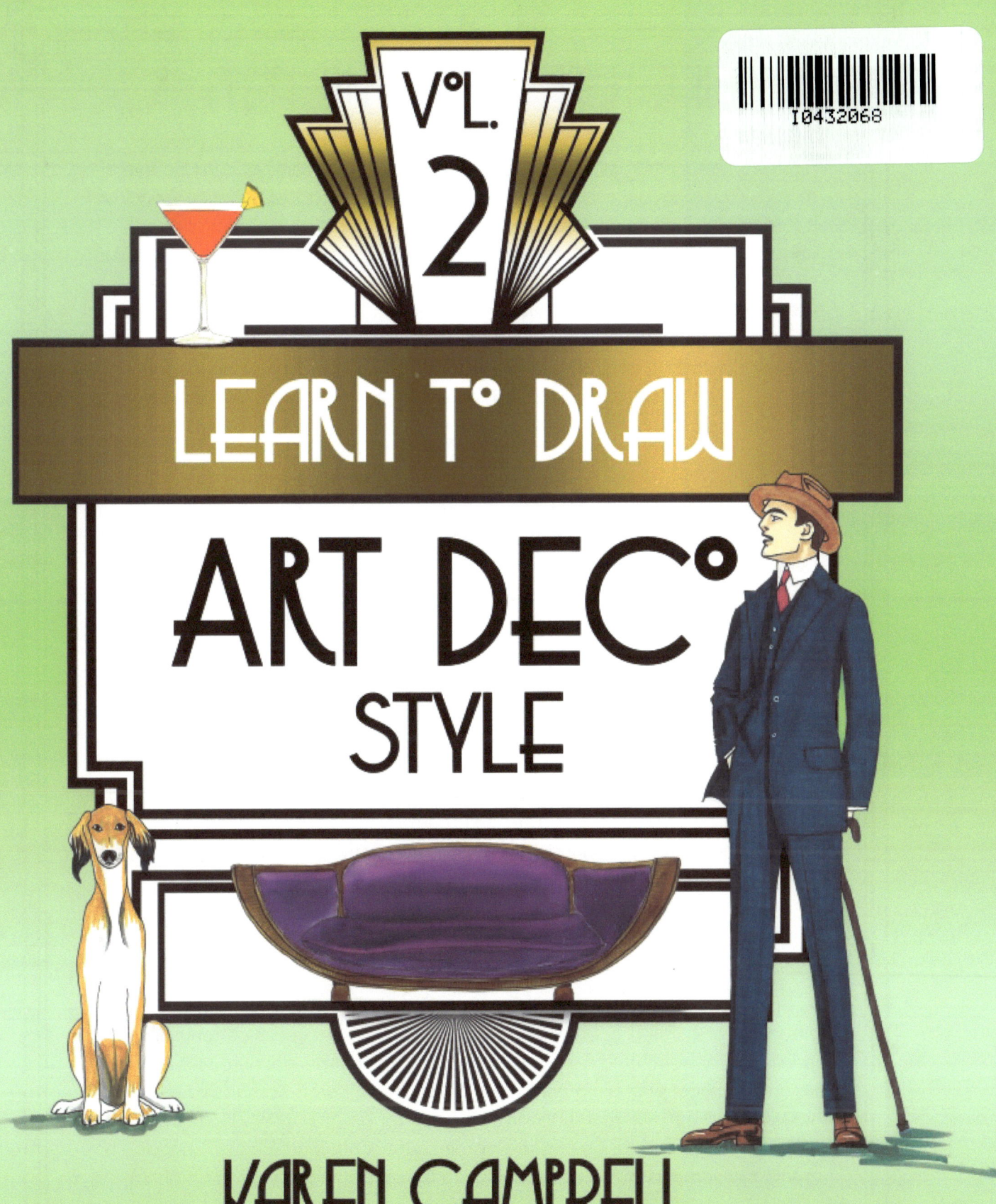

VOL. 2
LEARN TO DRAW
ART DECO STYLE

KAREN CAMPBELL

Return Once More to the Glamorous Jazz Age to Learn How to Create Stunning Drawings of Handsome Gents, Their Sleek Furry Companions, Unbelievably Realistic-Looking Home Decor, the Best of Speakeasy Cocktails and So Much More!

A WEE NOTE FROM THE AUTHOR...

I often joke to my husband, "Find me a book, show, or movie that involves a different time, costumes and/or accents and I'm IN." So frankly, I can't believe it took me this long to incorporate my love for all things fabulous, fictional and/or historical to influence my books! I've had such a blast drawing the ladies and jewels, dresses and shoes from this era, that there was no way that I could fit in all the rest, (and there's so much more goodness to cover)! And thus Volume II was born. I hope you enjoy drawing and coloring all the gents and dogs, cars, couches and cocktails as much as I did! They are every bit as fun as the ladies are to draw, which you'll soon discover; I do so hope you'll be brave and give them all a try! And to all my students at Awesome Art School, I love learning and creating with you!

I had to do a lot of research for this book and credit the following websites for providing additional factual information and/or inspiration: smithsonianmag.com, vintagedancer.com, fascinationstreetvintage.wordpress.com, thecoollist.com, gentlemansgazette.com, violetsvintagevault.wordpress.com, thevintagetraveler.wordpress.com, history.com, kegnbottle.com and glamourdaze.com.

For a list of my favorite art supplies: www.amazon.com/shop/karencampbellartist

Text and Illustrations Copyright © 2020 by Karen Campbell. All rights reserved.
Author, Illustrator, Publisher: Karen Campbell, Artist, LLC karencampbellartist.com
Cover Design: KT Design, LLC ktdesignllc.com
Editors: Linda Duvel and Mandi Brown trianglecreativegroup.com

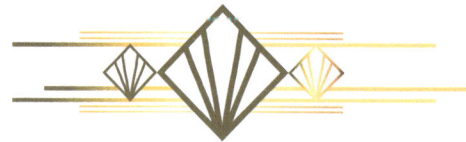

This book has been written and designed to aid the aspiring artist. Reproduction of work for at-home practice is permissible. Any art produced, electronically reproduced, or distributed from this publication for commercial purposes is forbidden without written content from the publisher, Karen Campbell, Artist, LLC. If you would like to use material from this book for any purpose outside of private use, prior written permission must be obtained by contacting the publisher at karen@awesomeartschool.com. Thank you for supporting the author's rights.

HAVE FUN!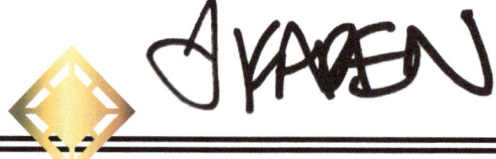

THE GENTS

Men's fashion 100 years ago is not that different from what some men wear to work and to very formal affairs today.

Men wore traditional 3 piece suits in dark colors like blue, grey and brown. Lighter shades didn't come into vogue until the mid 20's.
Vest styles were the most variable and were available in many contrasting colors, cuts and prints.
Hats were worn both during the day at work and with evening attire when out on the town. The Panama, Fedora, Homburg, Newsboy, Derby (bowler),
and Boater were the most popular styles and we will be drawing some of these as we draw our dapper dudes!

Standard formal evening attire was a full tuxedo complete with tailcoat (white or black), dress shirt, vest, white or black bow tie, overcoat and patent leather shoes.

Let's draw some chaps to accompany the ladies we drew in Volume I, shall we?

THE QUADRANT METHOD

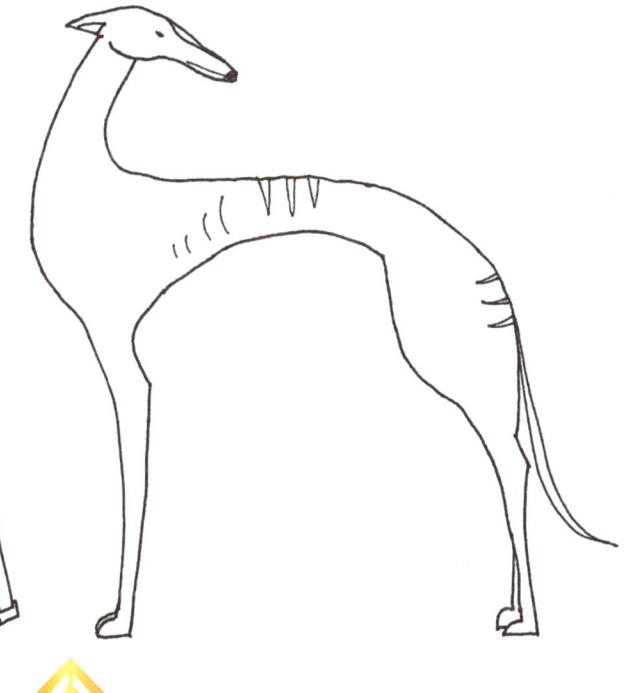

Before we begin coloring our first man, we need to draw him. Luckily, I've recently come up with a VERY easy system, that I call my **Quadrant** method, which makes it super easy to draw figures! Figures are normally pretty difficult, but don't worry, we will draw them together.

You will need the following supplies and then we will begin:

1) Ruler
2) Tracing Paper
3) Pencil
4) This reference outline of the man

That's it! Collect your things and meet me on the next page.

THE "CHARACTER CONTAINER"

We will begin by making a rectangular "container" for our dapper fellow here. To do so, follow the simple steps.

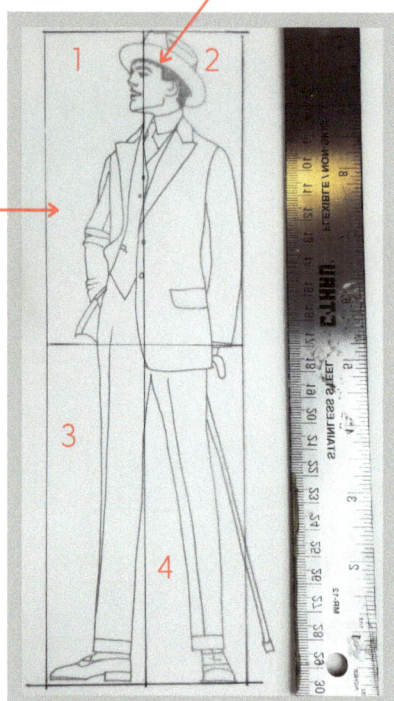

reference under trace

trace paper on top

Step 1. Take your piece of trace paper and lay it over our man here. You could even draw these lines over the reference in the book if you wanted to!

Step 2. With your ruler, draw (and measure) a rectangle that fits him exactly.

Step 3. Divide that rectangle in half both vertically and horizontally so your set-up looks like this photo on the right.

You've just created the first 4 **Quadrants** (numbered here in red).
Each line we draw is going to become a guideline (or reference line) that will help us draw our own gentleman on our own papers.

Step 4. Add 2 more horizontal lines.

Step 5. Assess your new **Quadrants** (now you have 8). Do you think these are enough guidelines to help you draw him on your own paper? No? I don't think so either. Not a problem; we can easily add more.

Step 6. Divide your 8 **Quadrants** again, in places that you think you'll need more help drawing. Turn the page and I'll show you exactly what I mean and what this looks like.

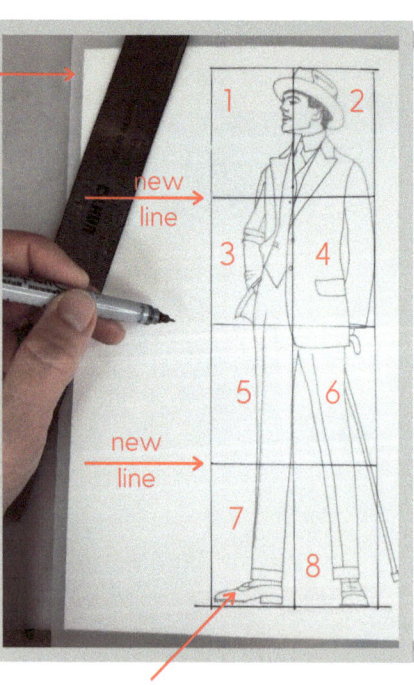

trace paper

new line

new line

reference under

Step 7. Using your measurements from the original "character container," recreate the same **Quadrants** on your own paper. To make this easy, draw them the exact same size (so 1:1 scale). If you want to make your drawing a different size, simply adjust the math accordingly and go!

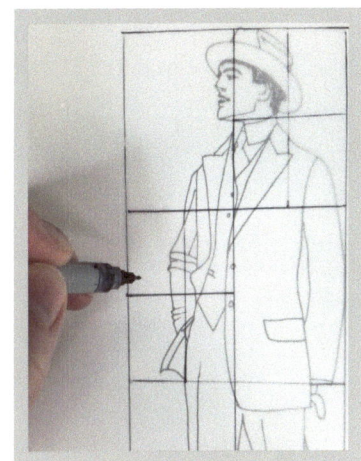

Adding more is super easy! Just freehand them in as needed.

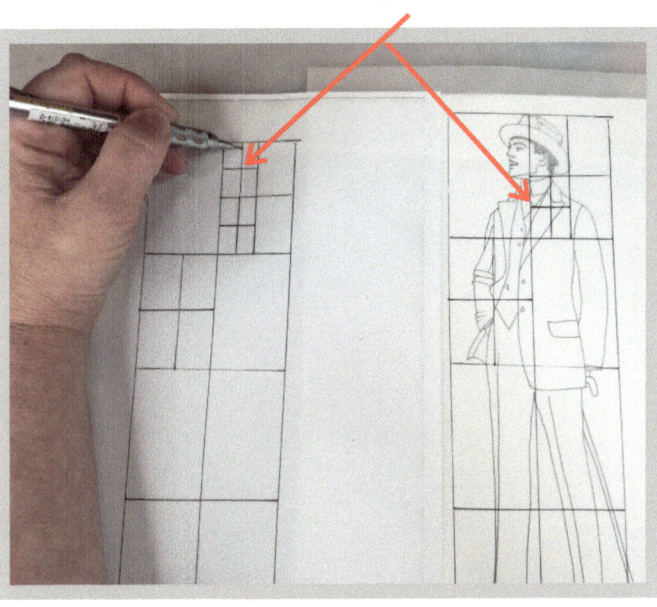

Step 8. Work slowly, rectangle by rectangle, and begin to transfer what you see on the reference onto your own paper. Use the guidelines to help you judge proper spacing between objects, lines and elements. Continue this way until the entire figure has been drawn.

NOTE: The type of paper you choose to draw on is extremely important. If you plan to color this man in the same way that I will be showing you, you'll want to be drawing on special watercolor paper. I'm working on Fabriano Hot Press Watercolor Paper. It is smooth, so great for drawing, but also specially made to accept water mediums. If you're using colored pencils, then any paper will do. If you're using markers, then Bristol or cardstock would be the ideal choice! Once you have your paper ready, you can begin recreating the **Quadrants** on your paper.

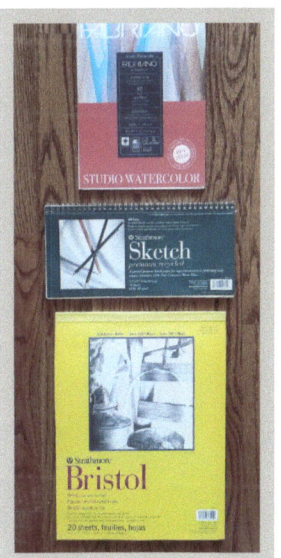

Step 9. As you draw your object bit by bit, just worry about drawing the general shapes at first. Don't get caught up in the details quite yet. Your first priority is just to sketch the overall shapes in and make sure all your proportions look correct when you compare them to the original reference. Then, after you've gotten the overall shape, should you go in and refine the details.

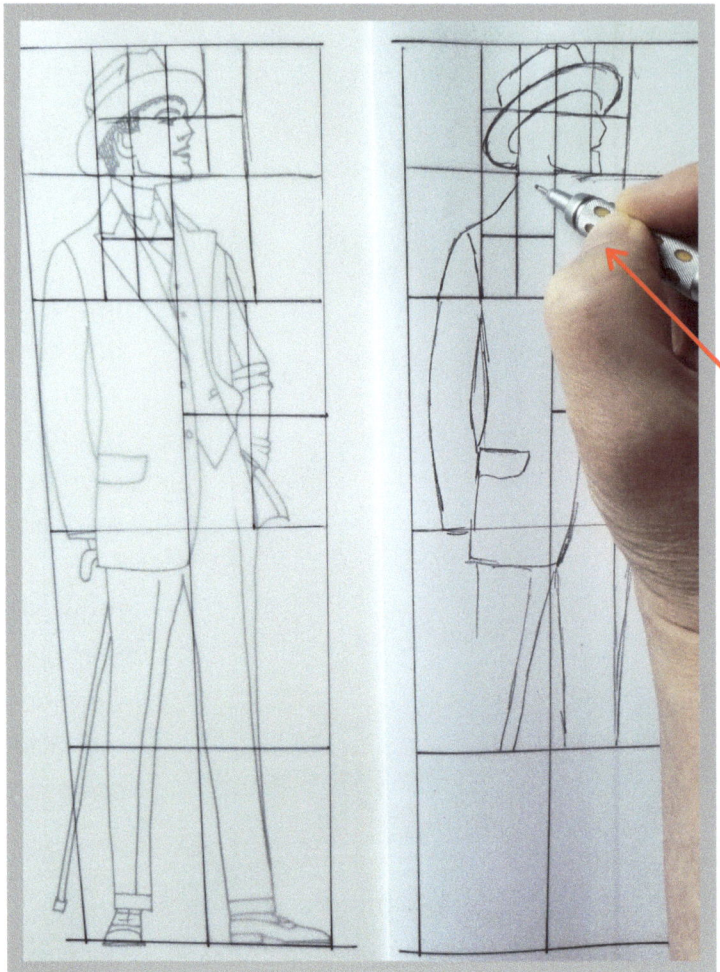

The objective is to make your Quadrants **and your drawing** look EXACTLY like the reference (shown left).

Quadrants, lines and details should all be in a 1:1 ratio and drawn the same. At least that's the goal!!

Just try your best! You can do it!

I ended up adding even MORE to help myself out. Do the same if you need to!

If this concept is still a little fuzzy, you can watch the video so you can see exactly how the **Quadrant** system works in action! It's on YouTube so don't worry; it's free! Just type the following URL into your browser and press play!
http://bit.ly/quadrantsystem

ALM°ST THERE!

Step 10. All you have to do now is fine tune your drawing, outline your dapper dude with your favorite fineliner (I like Copic multiliners but any fine tip pen will work!), and erase your guidelines! Once you've completed the drawing, get ready to color!

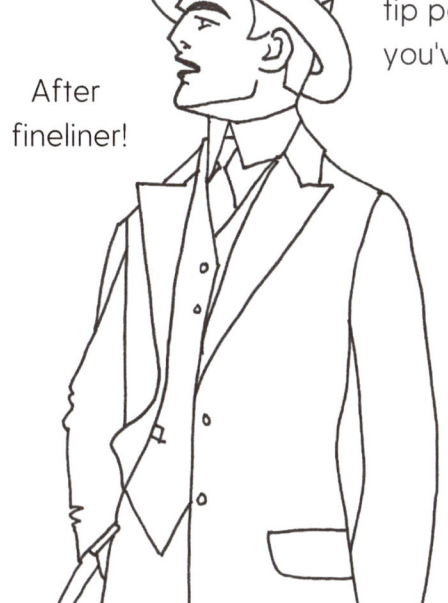

After fineliner!

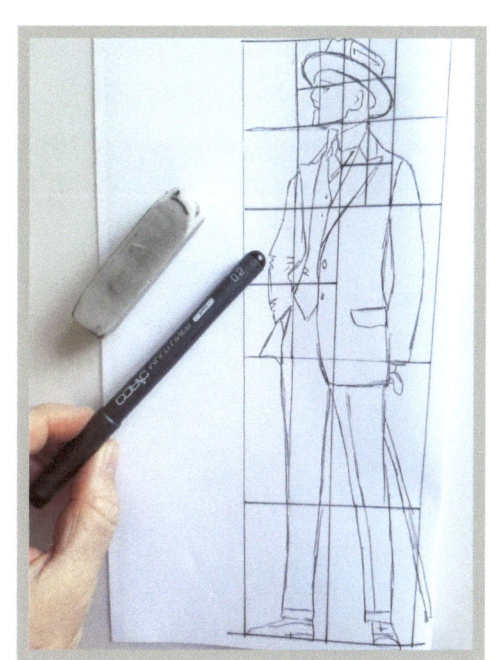

Helpful Hints:

1. Sketch your **Quadrant** lines lightly, so that when you erase, they go away completely.
2. If you want a cleaner copy of the outline, you can trace! Hold your drawing up to a window and tape a blank sheet of paper on top. Trace with your fineliner! Done!

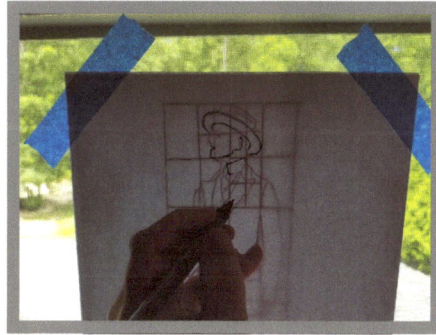

After the outline is drawn with your fineliner, and all **Quadrant** lines have been erased, you are ready to finish him! Markers are great for creating the look of cloth texture. Here's a simple tip that will help you create the same look. You can see the difference if you look at his coat versus his pants. I started by coloring in his entire suit with blue Copic marker, making long vertical brush strokes. Then go back and do a second layer, this time using horizontal brush strokes.

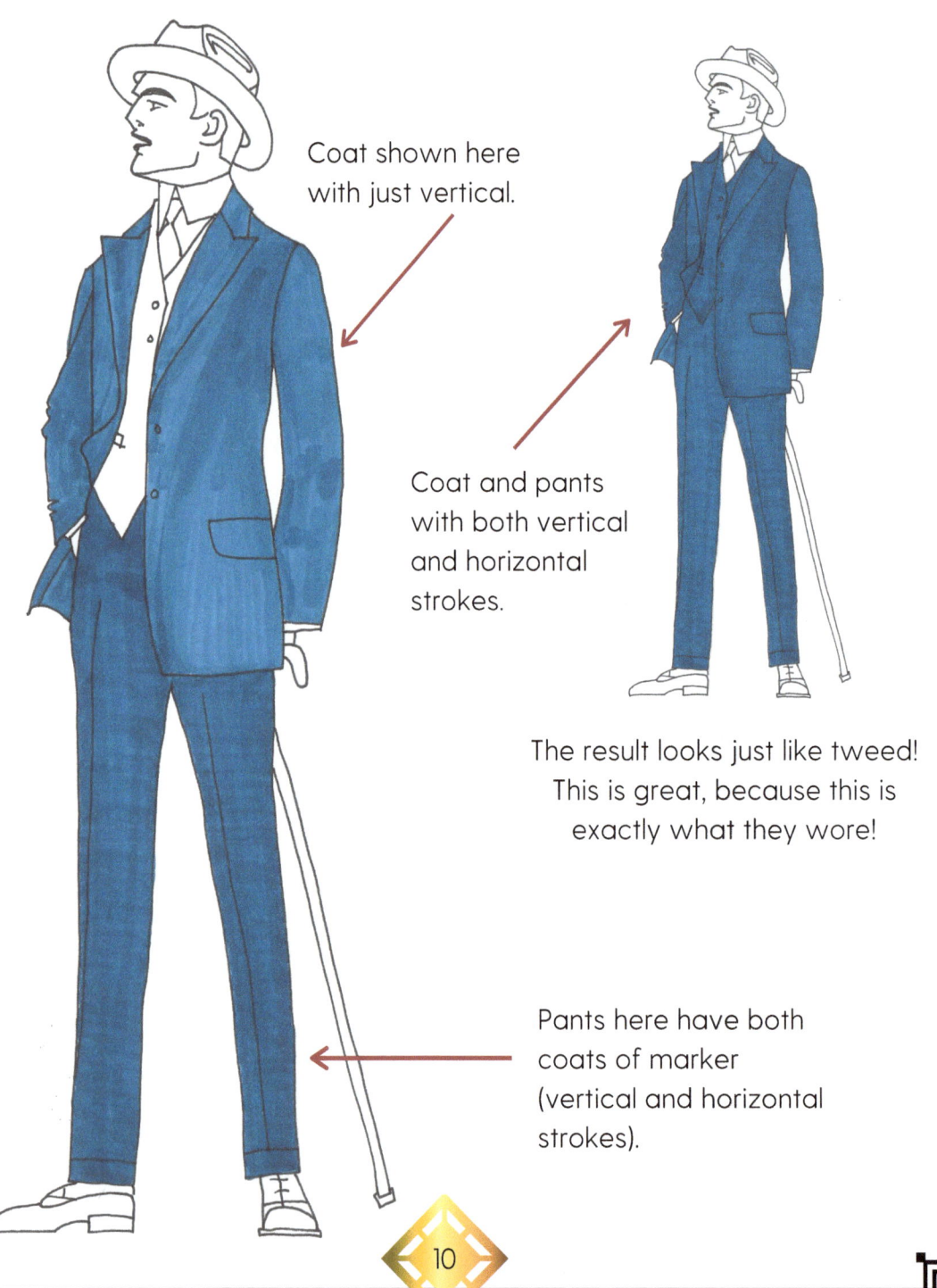

Coat shown here with just vertical.

Coat and pants with both vertical and horizontal strokes.

The result looks just like tweed! This is great, because this is exactly what they wore!

Pants here have both coats of marker (vertical and horizontal strokes).

Every drawing has an imaginary light source. Great looking shading starts with a light source off to one side. For this drawing, pretend there is one on right (see bulb). This light will cast shadows off to the left and inside the fabric folds closest to the body (as the light source cannot penetrate those areas).

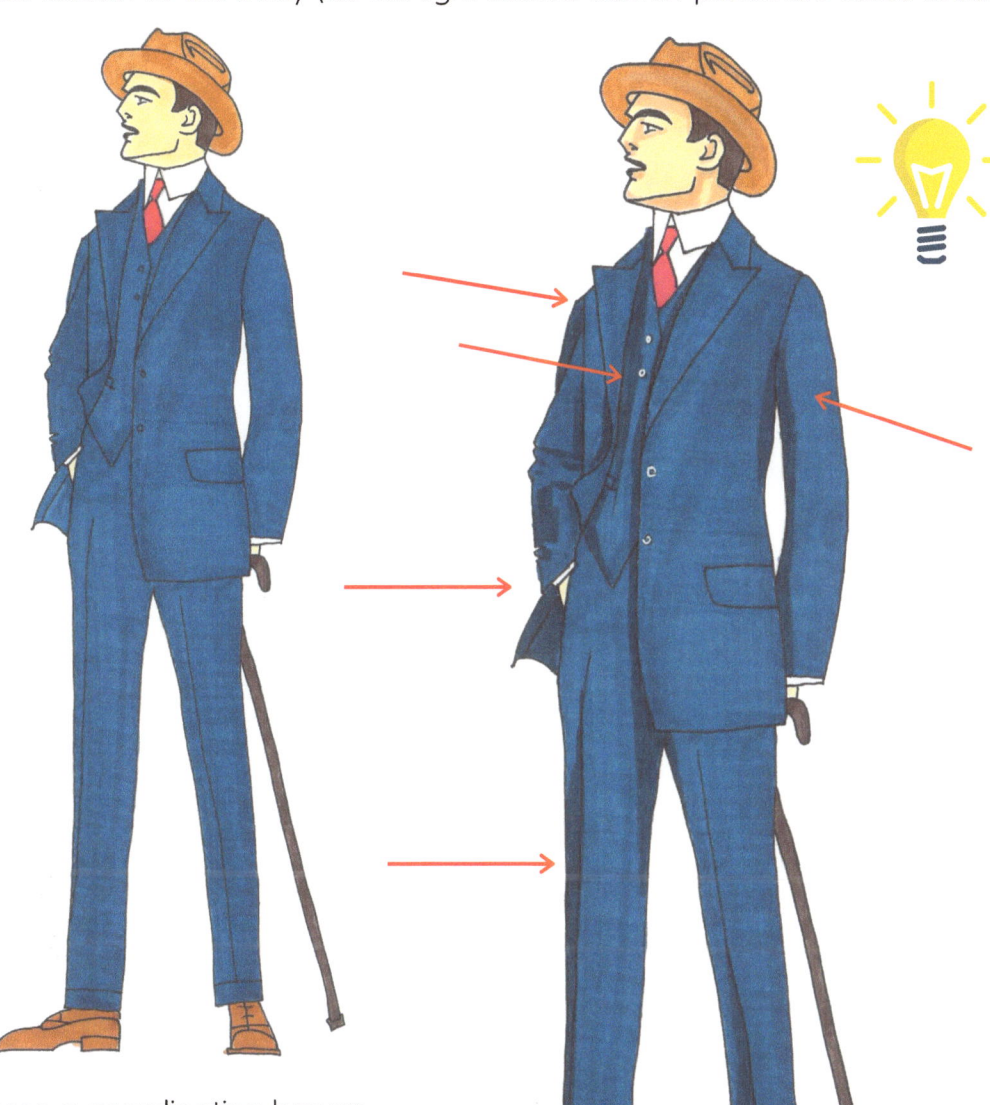

Choose a coordinating brown for the hat and shoes. Or don't! Still, the look is rather flat until you add the subtle shading. Choose a dark grey and add streaks of it in the places you see in the next step (see red arrows). Use a white gel pen to highlight the buttons.

In these side-by-side images, you can really see what a difference those hightlights and shadows make to add dimension to your drawing.

You can always use the **Quadrant** method to draw absolutely anything. Or, you can create your own guidelines like in this Greyhound example.

Step 1. Create rectangle to set the overall size.

Step 2. At the halfway point sketch a curved line. Then add another above it.

Step 3. Add more curving lines for the neck/head and legs.

Step 4. Add head and complete legs.

Step 5. Add ear, bend in the neck, paws and tail (in red).

Step 6. Erase rectangle, guidelines and outline with fineliner pen.

Step 7. Color as desired!

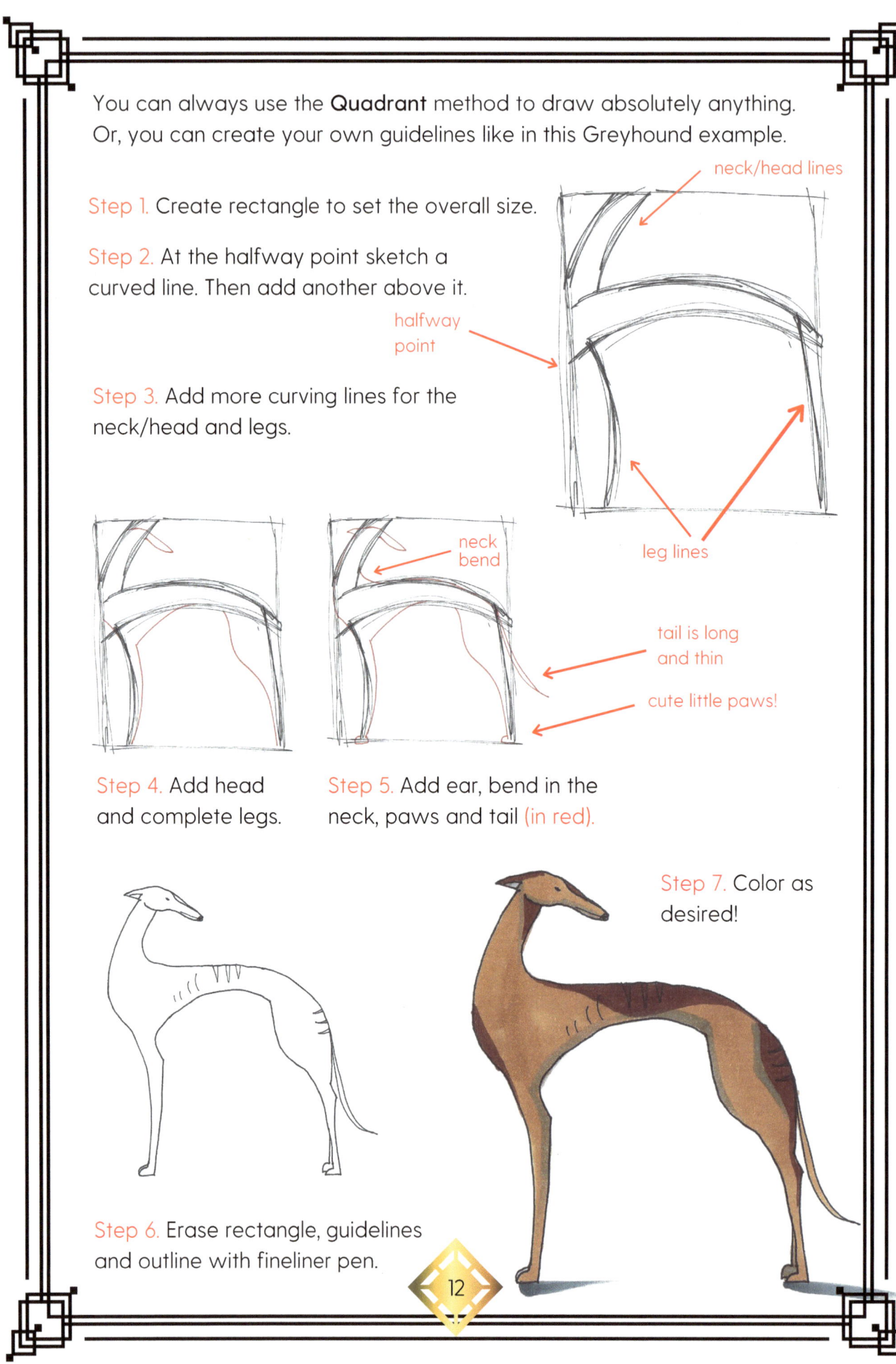

CHAP AND MATE

I'm a HUGE Peaky Blinders fan (TV show) and this book would not be complete without a chain smoking, laid back, tough guy wearing a newsboy cap! Dachshunds were very popular in this era as well, so he is here too.
Use the **Quadrant** method to draw the outline for the man, and the step-by-step instructions on the following page to draw his little buddy.

This drawing was inspired by a painting created in 1921 by J. C. Leyendecker. He was a very talented and prolific artist who created hundreds of illustrations for advertising companies and magazines.

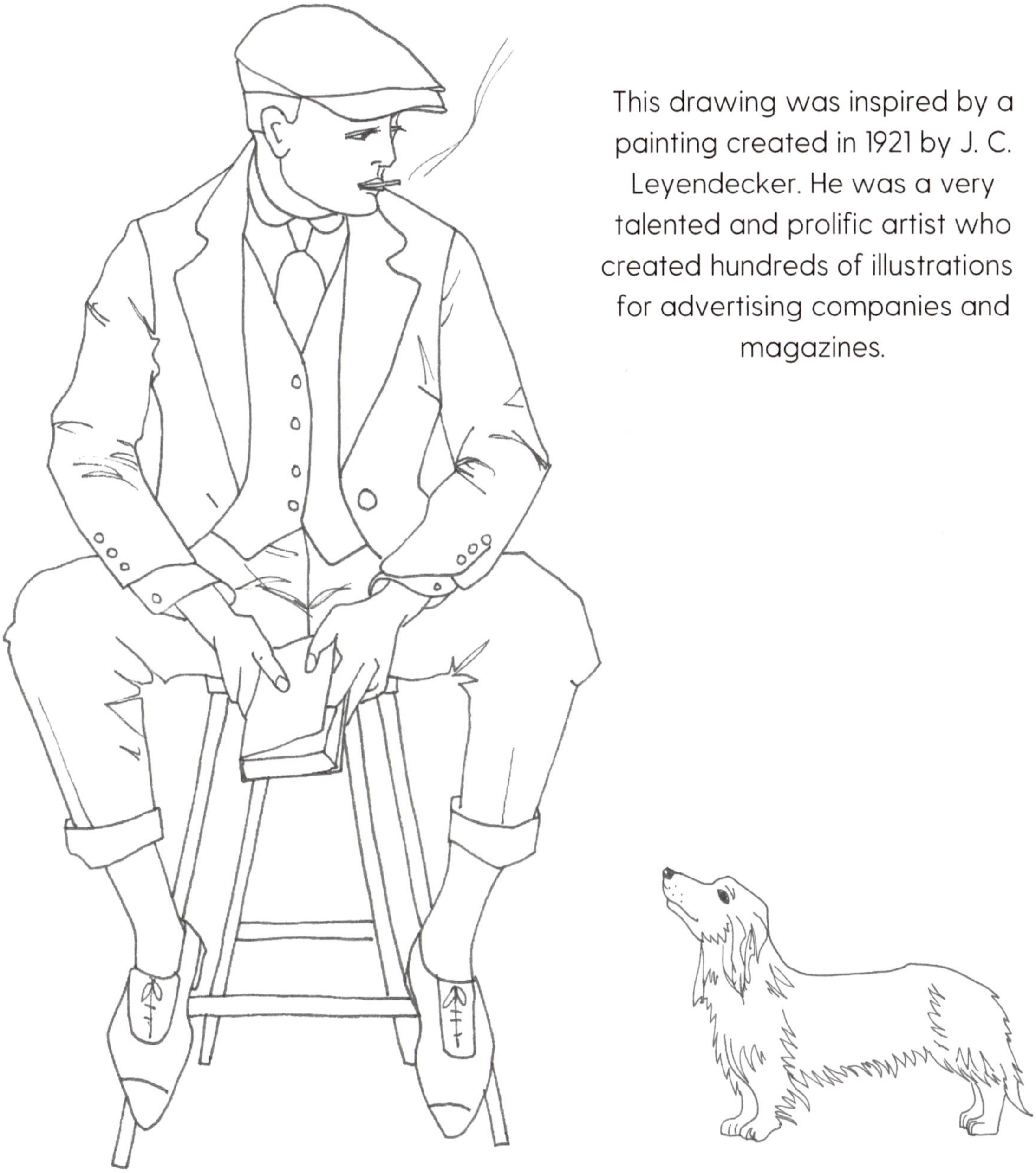

QUADRANTS MAKE IT EASY

Don't let the fact that the man is sitting deter you from diving right into the **Quadrant** method. Again, this system works on anything and everything. It is easier to draw the general shapes first, and disregard the clothes wrinkles and fine details until after you've establish the drawing.

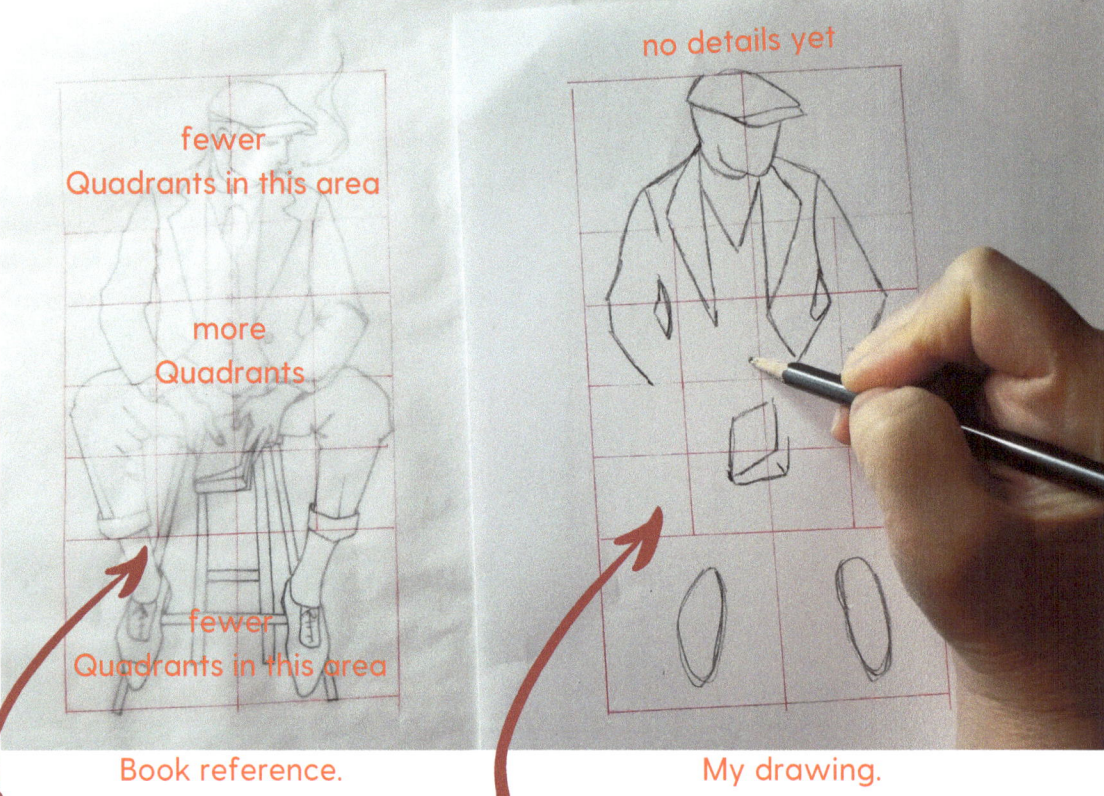

Book reference.

My drawing.

You can see my trace paper on top of the reference. I drew my **Quadrants** in red.

Draw as many (or as few) guidelines as you need to help you!

I needed more help in the center areas of the drawing (where it is busier) so I added more **Quadrants** there. I left the other areas more open as I thought I had enough information to draw without further help or more lines.

Your set-up should look similar.

In this example, I recreated the **Quadrants** on my own drawing paper in red. I would recommend drawing them in pencil so you can erase them when you're through! I just wanted to make sure you saw them clearly for this example.

DRAWING THE DOG

Step 1. Draw a rectangle. This allows you to determine the scale of the dog (specifically, the height and length). If you draw the rectangle and it looks too large, you can easily resize it without having to disrupt your whole drawing since all you have at this point is the box, and not the whole dog.

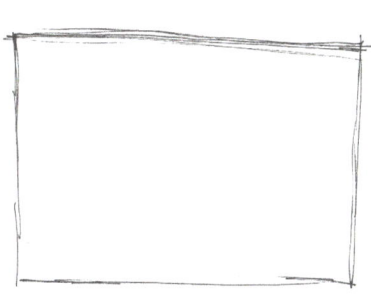

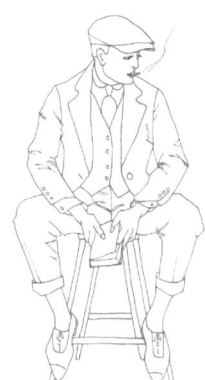

Woah!! That Daschund looks way too big. Now is the time to make the rectangle smaller.

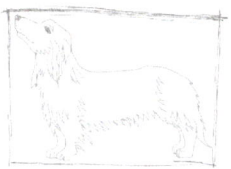

Step 2. Once you have the rectangle at the size you want, rough in the following shapes. You may add additional guidelines to help you determine the correct placement and size of the circles and lines.

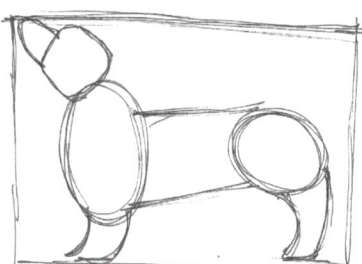
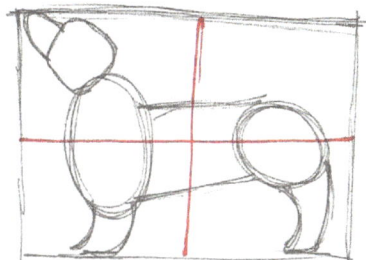

Look familiar? This is the **Quadrant** method at work! Only on a smaller scale.

Step 3. Refine the shape of the dog.   **Step 4** Erase the guidelines and outline.

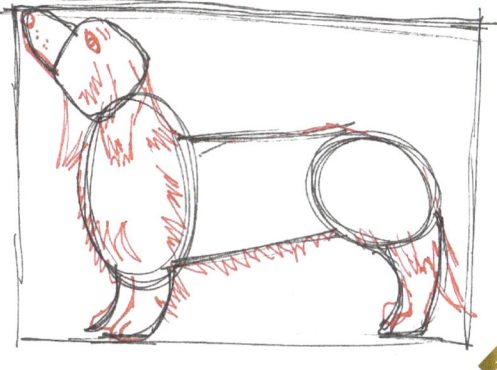
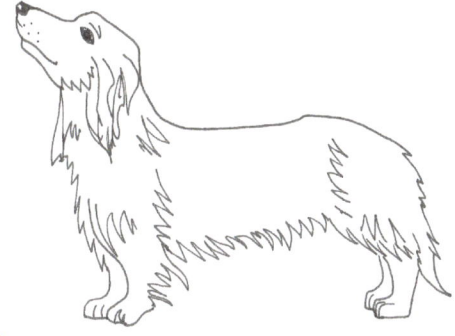

COLORING THE DOG

Have fun coloring your animals! You can experiment with different mediums to see how it affects the overall look!

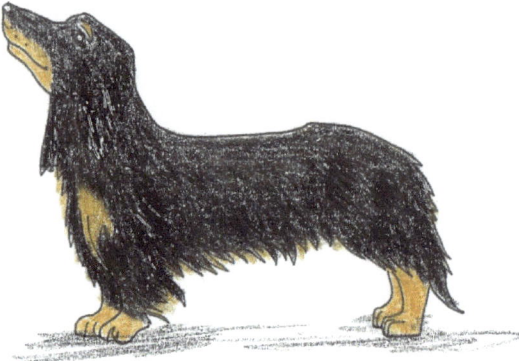

Colored pencils

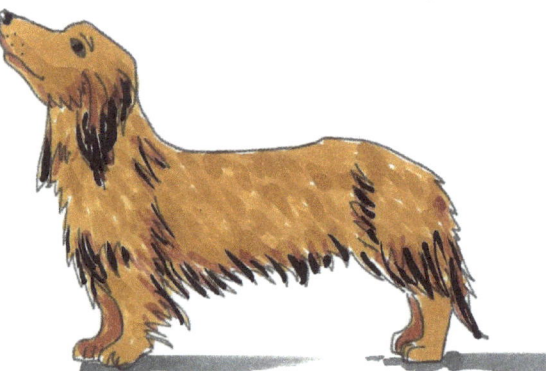

Copic Markers

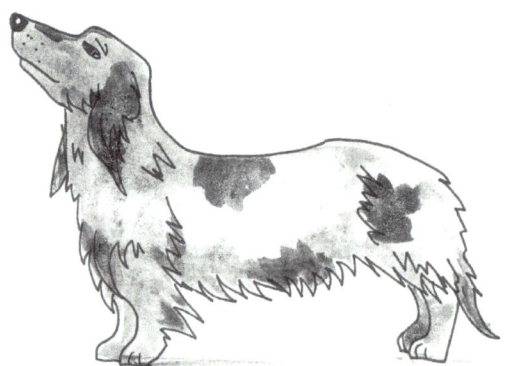

Watercolors

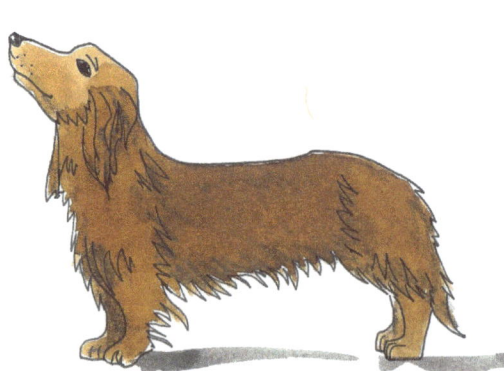

Fountain Pen Ink

INKING IT IN.

There's no right or wrong way to color in a drawing. Just make sure that whatever you decide, you start with the right paper. I cannot stress this enough.

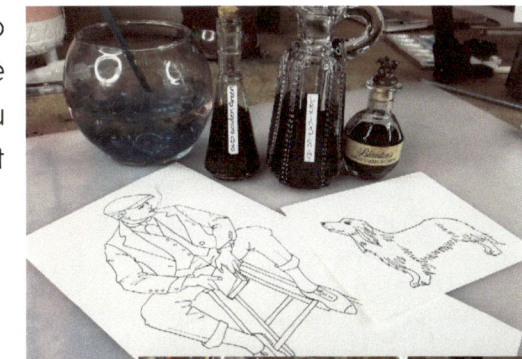

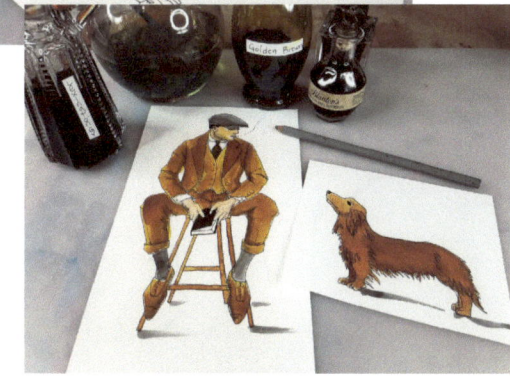

My drawing was done on Fabriano Hotpress Watercolor Paper and colored in using Noodler's Fountain Pen ink with a soft 3B graphite pencil for subtle shading.

EVENING ATTIRE

Men were required to don their formal attire much more frequently then they are today. It is therefore quite appropriate that we learn how to draw them!

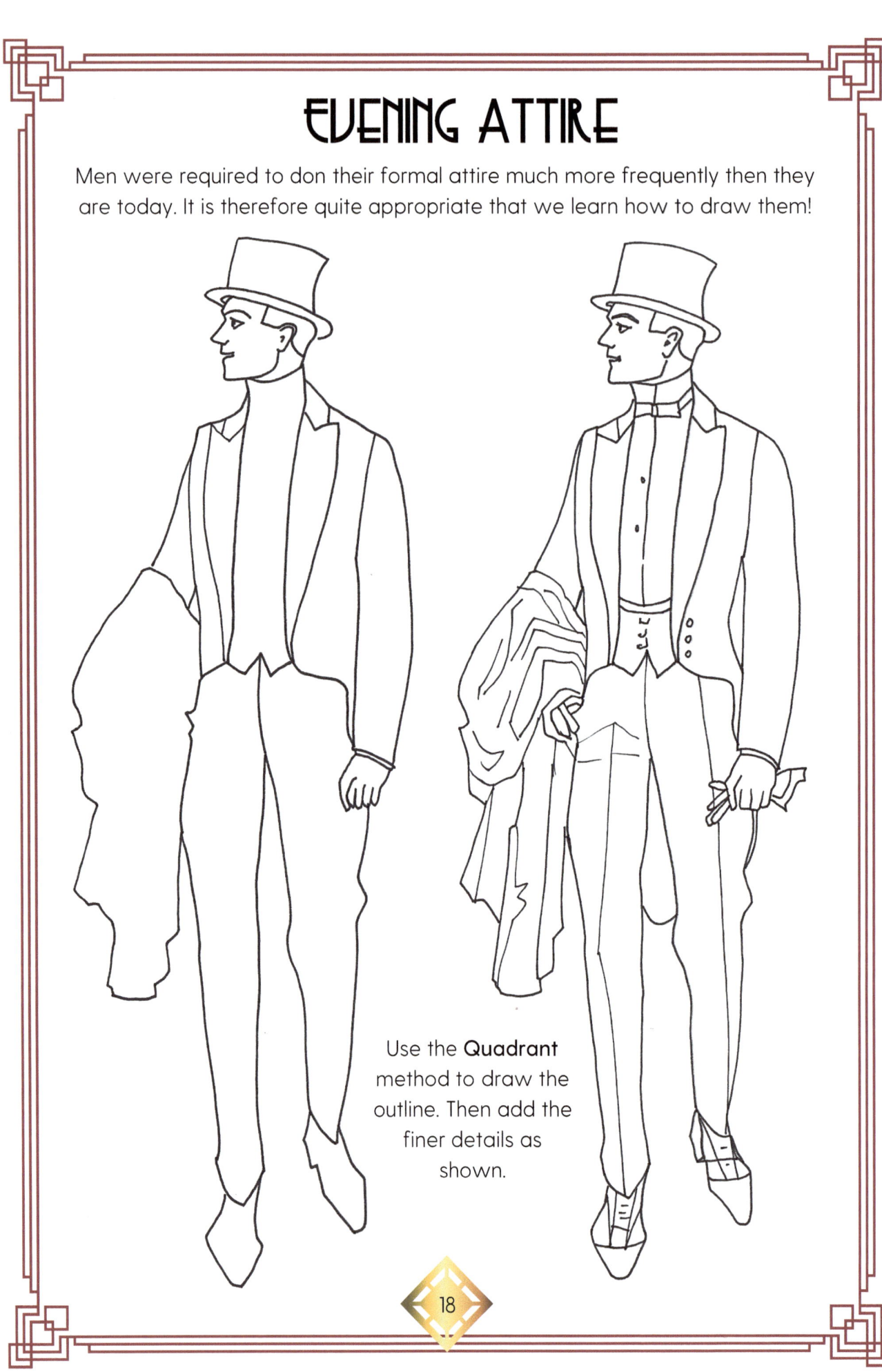

Use the **Quadrant** method to draw the outline. Then add the finer details as shown.

A sure fire way to color black tuxedos is to use a combination of black and the darkest shade of grey you can find. Use the grey to do an all over color. Then use the true black in very specific places. In this drawing, we are pretending the light source is coming from the left, so the shadows, will fall mainly to the right.

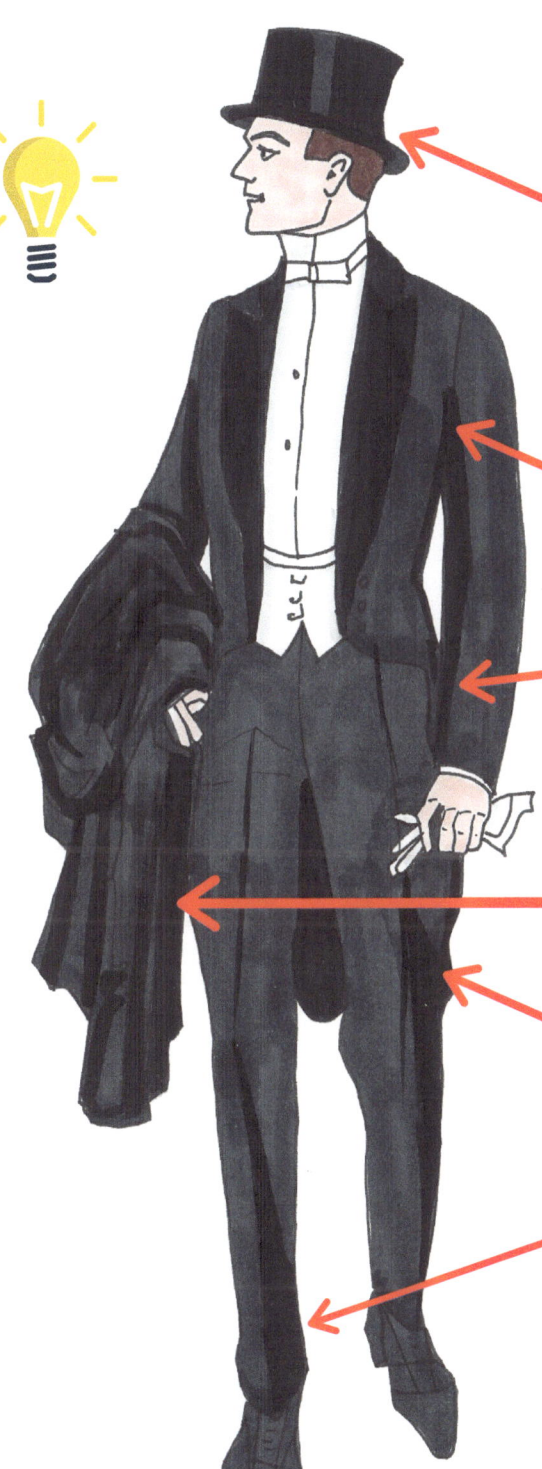

Use true black on the top hat, but leave a strip of grey. We will be highlighting that soon!

Add black to the inside of the sleeves and lapels.

Color black haphazardly to show the dark creases in the folded over coat.

Use black to accentuate the fine crease down the pant legs. Then continue the shading off to the right side (because again, the light source is shining on his left side).

BLACK 'R WHITE

Thanks to Edward, Prince of Wales, who was responsible for setting many fashion trends for men in the 1920's, white tuxedo jackets became fashionable.

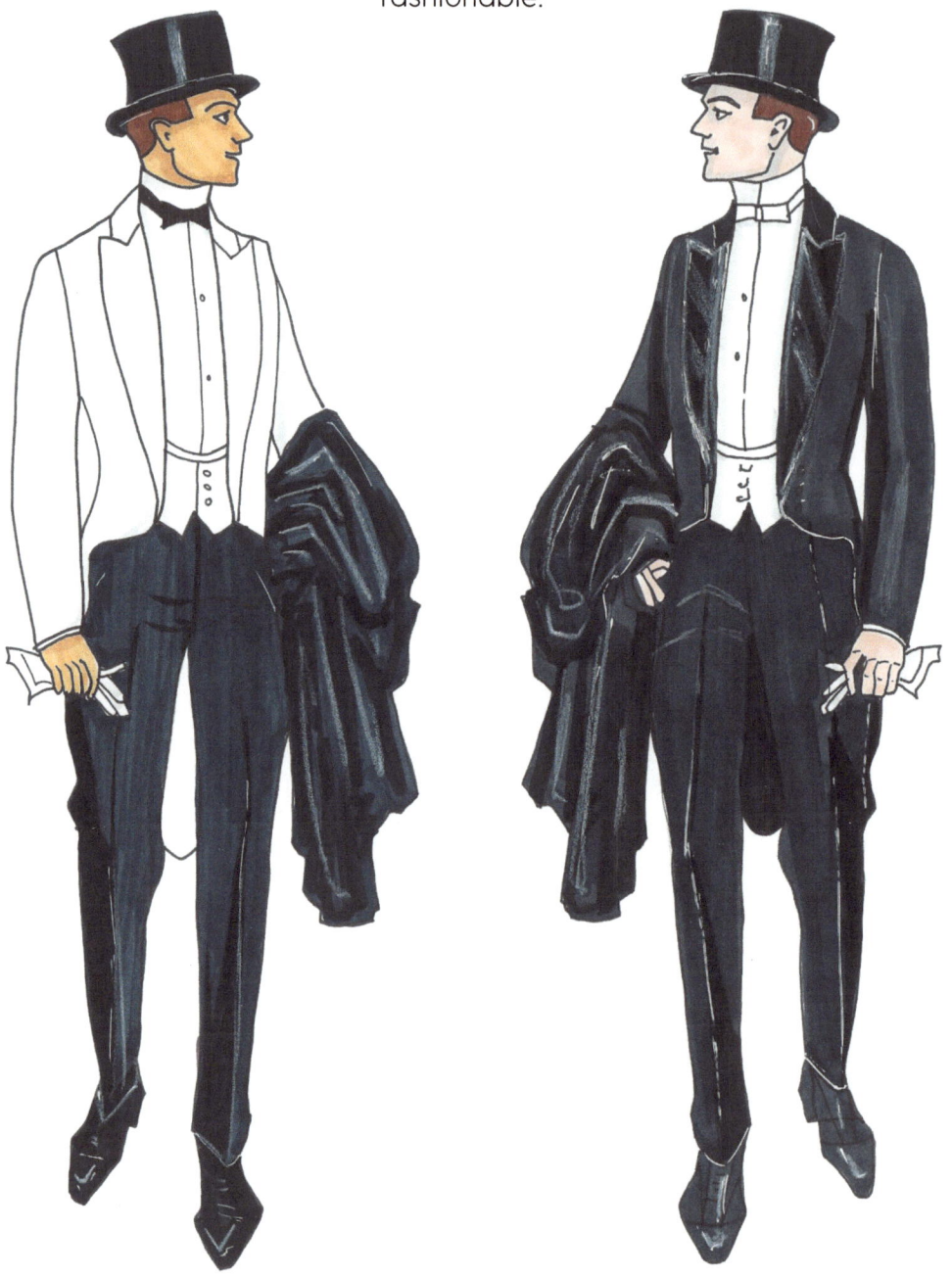

With a white pencil and/or a white gel pen, add pops of white to the creases in the pants, the lapels of the black tux top (which gives the appearance of a "sheen", indicative of a satiny fabric), and on the shoes, to give the look of patent leather.

MEN'S OUTERWEAR

Men's overcoats look very similar to what they look like today, the only difference being that in the 20's the coats were tailored to fit snugly, and in the 30's the coats became very boxy and roomy.

In this drawing our gentlemen is accompanied by his Borzoi friend. This was a very popular breed and was often depicted in the artwork of this time. Borzois are large, graceful and gentle breeds with the body of a greyhound...only furry!

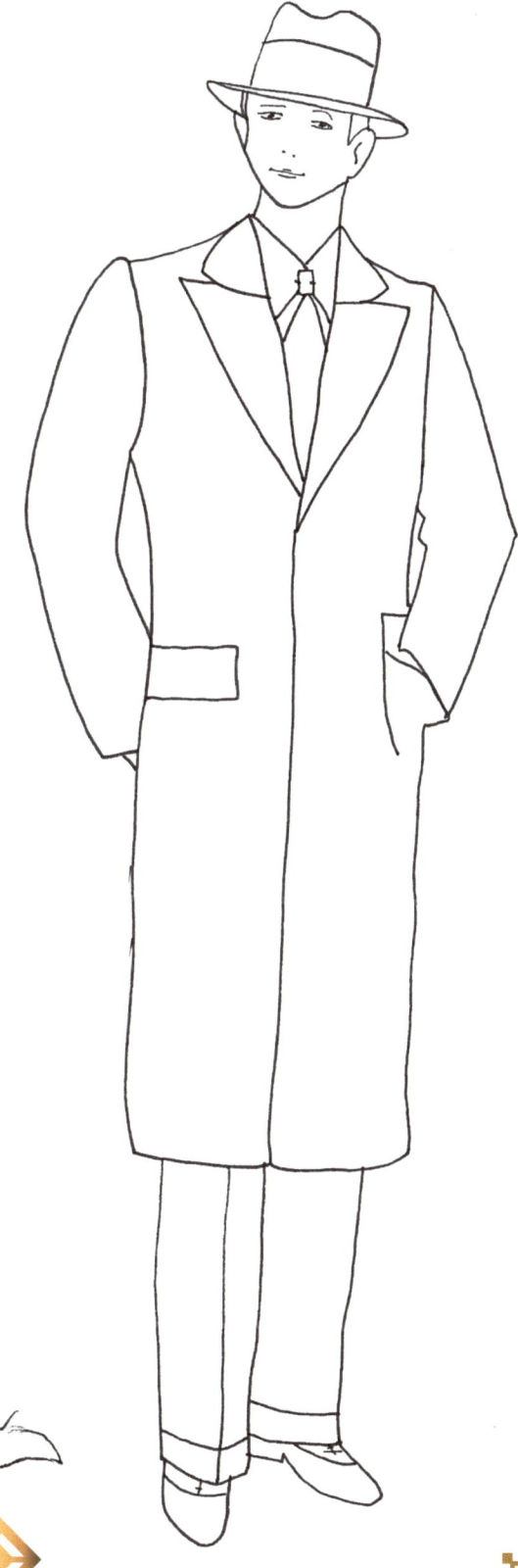
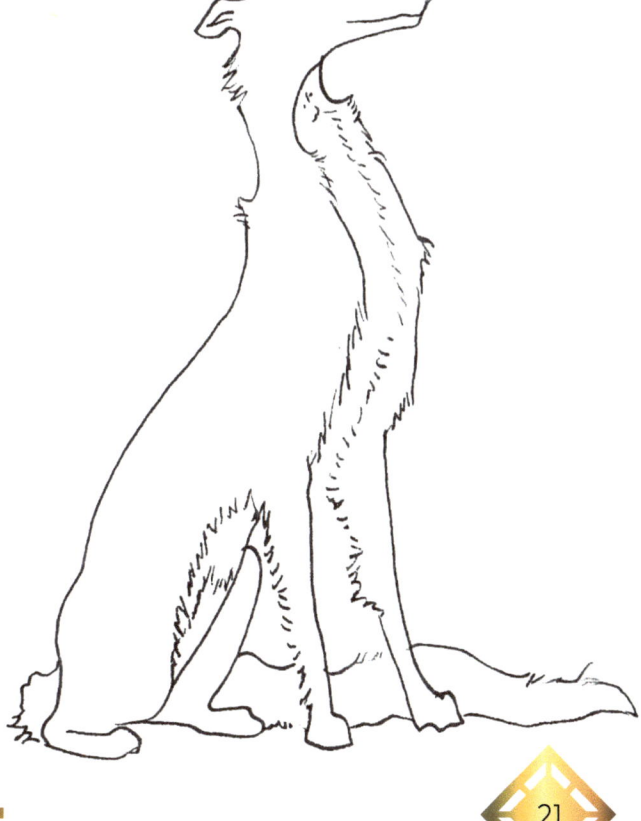

QUADRANT METHOD FOR ALL!

As always, to create this genteel pair, get out your tracing paper and pencils and let's begin. The man figure will have a tall rectangle and the steps to draw his gorgeous dog will look like this:

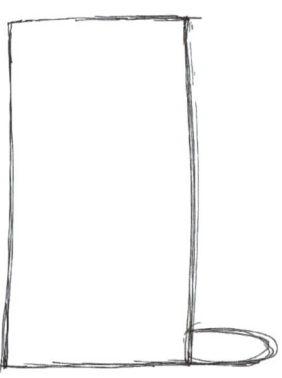

Step 1: Set up the rectangle for the dog. I'm leaving the tail out of the rectangle for this one and just drawing the length in as shown.

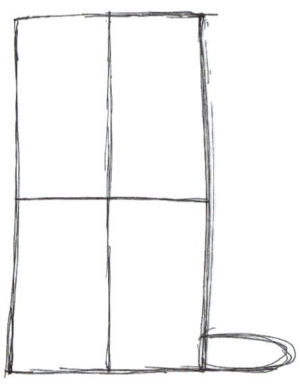

Step 2: Since the shape of the dog is pretty simple, I am only setting up 4 **Quadrants**. If you need more, draw them in!

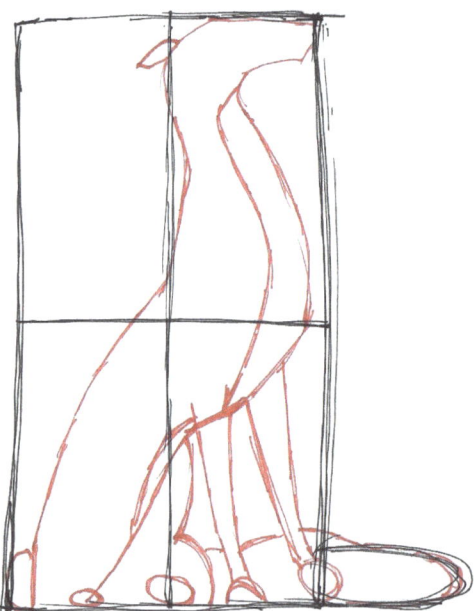

Step 3: Draw in the general outline of the body, ears, legs and tail.

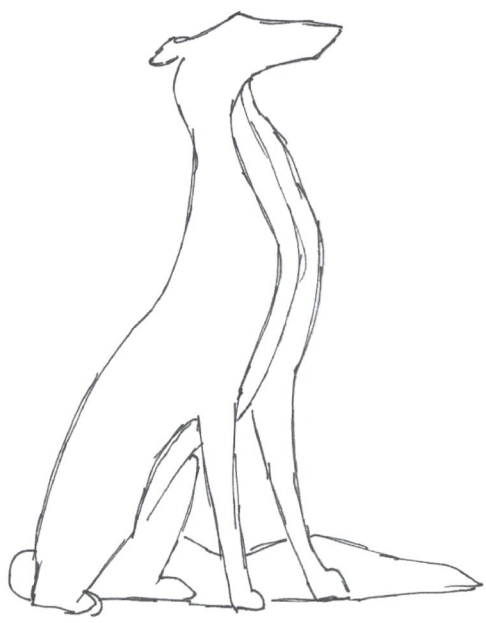

Step 4: Erase your guidelines.

FINAL DOG DETAILS

Now, if you like, you can replace some of the more solid lines with furry lines! This is very similar to the way we rendered the fur coat in the women's fashion chapter in Volume 1.

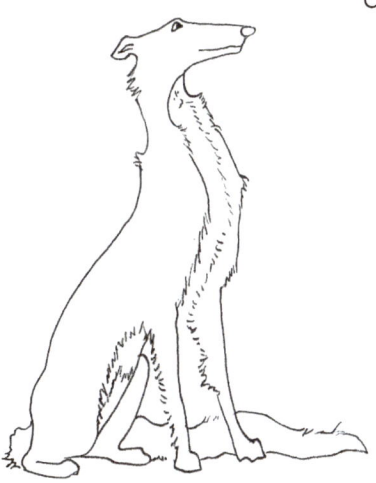

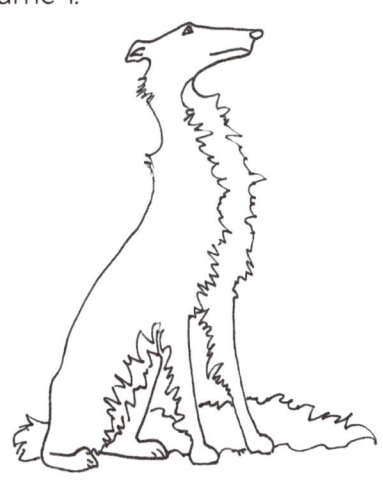

Step 5: Add small lines to indicate the fur coat.

Step 6: Make him as fluffy as you wish by making larger squiggle-like lines!

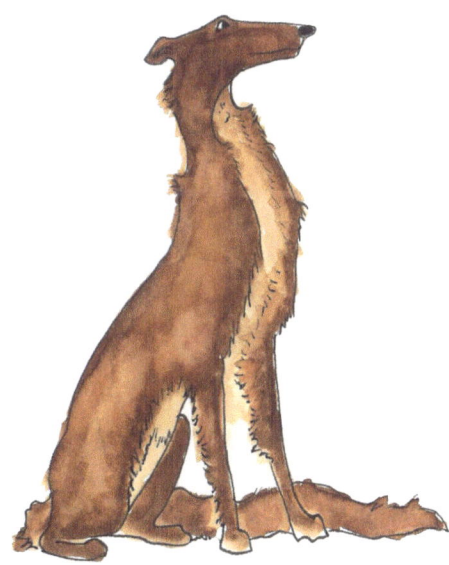

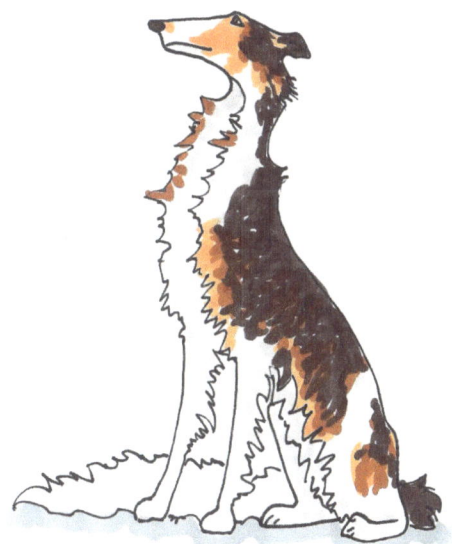

Step 7: Color in your Borzoi any way you please! On the left I am coloring with a Watercolor marker. On the right, Copic markers. Borzois come in a few gorgeous coat colors from light golden brown, to solid white, black, and spotted! You can easily look up images on the internet to get inspired!

RENDERING CLOTHES

For this project I am using watercolor markers and colored pencils to create a realistic clothing look!

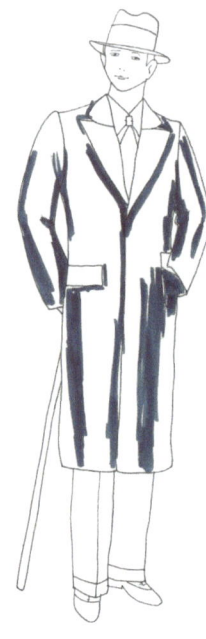
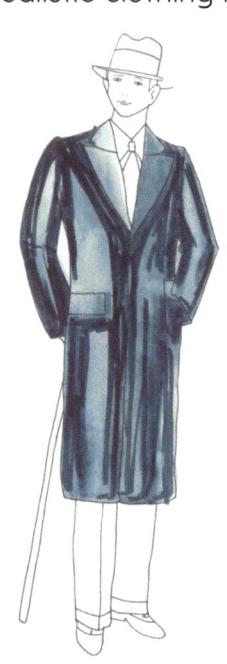
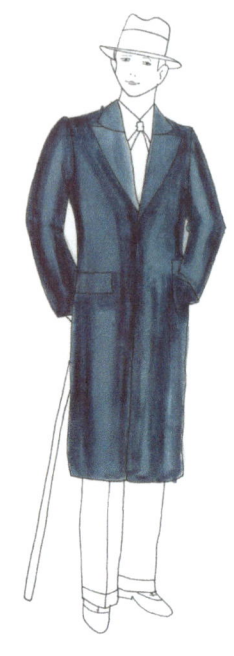

Step 1: Apply marker to the suit.

Step 2: Add water with a damp brush to all of the marker. Let dry. Then add more marker.

Step 3: Add more water.

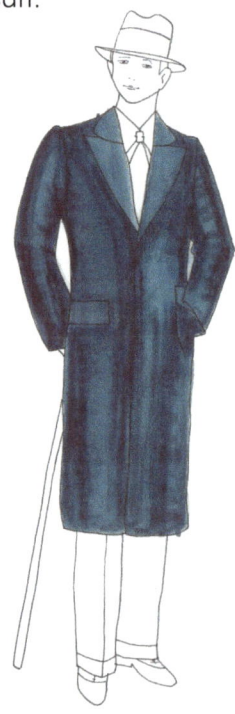
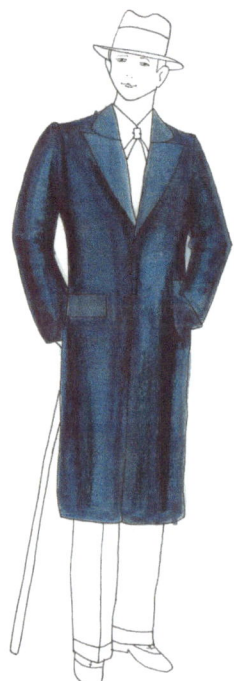

Step 5: Apply marker, but this time, with short horizontal strokes.

Step 6: Add water again with a damp brush.

COLOR PENCIL MAGIC

Step 7. Now that the base marker coat is finished, we will be adding a layer of colored pencils. For this step, you need to choose colored pencils that are very similar to your marker colors. Using a light touch, color over the entire coat with a colored pencil using short, horizontal strokes.

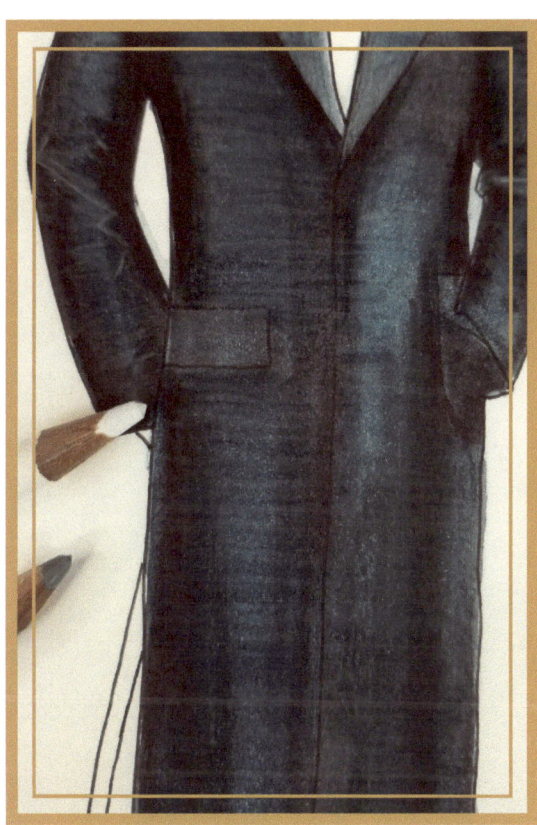

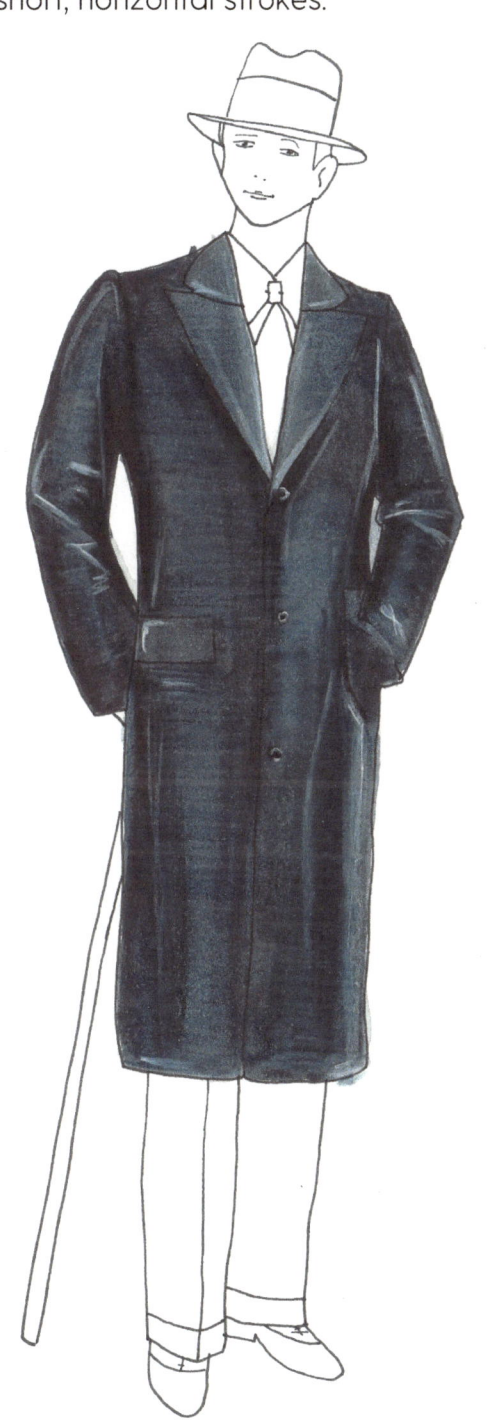

Step 8: Using the same technique, add highlights in light grey (or light blue would work too). If you're not happy with the result, you still have time to make corrections. You can do so by repeating the darker colors.

Step 9: Add highlights in white pencil and/or pen to the areas shown.

GRAND FINALE

Complete the gentlemen by using the same approach for the hat and pants.

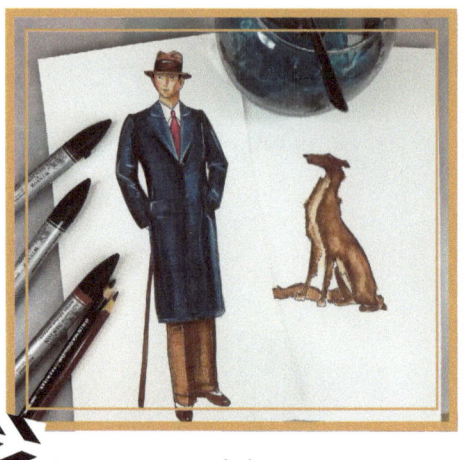

I've captured the entire project on video for you! You can watch it here (it's free):

http://bit.ly/1920gentleman

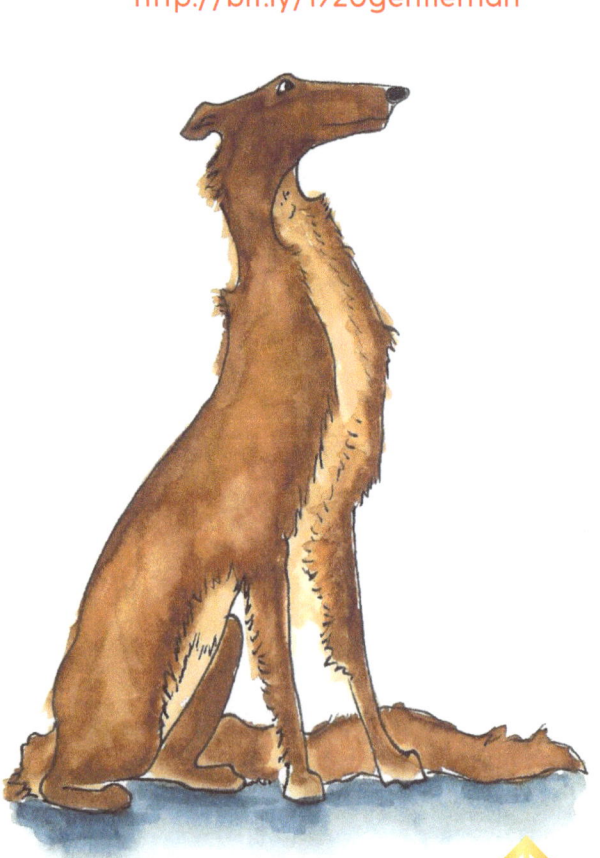

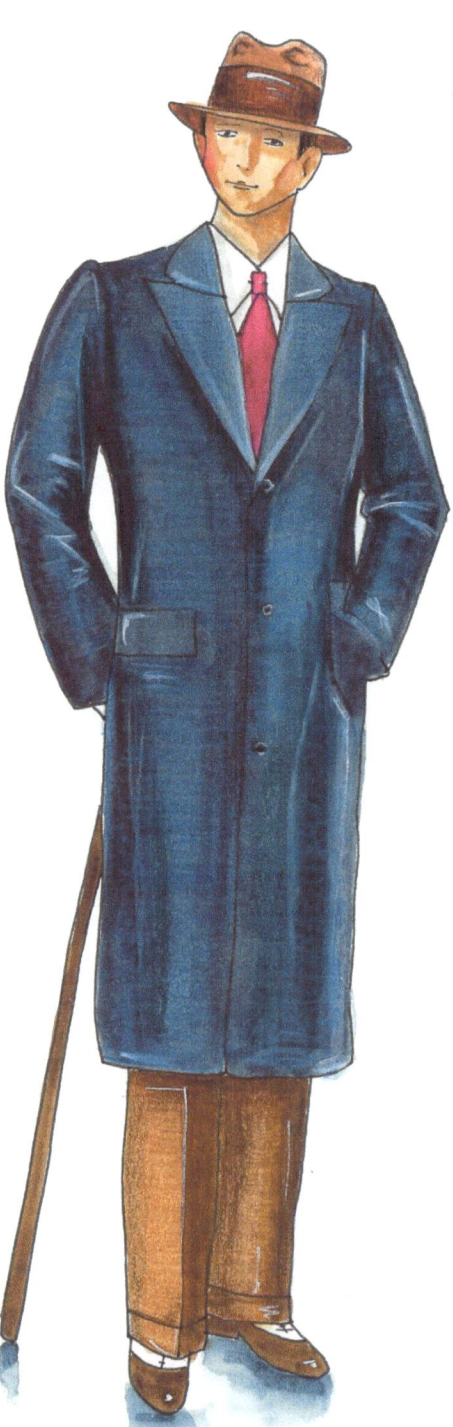

GET INSPIRED!

It's so fun to draw dudes from this era! Go online and search 1920's gangsters or musicians to find great pics!!

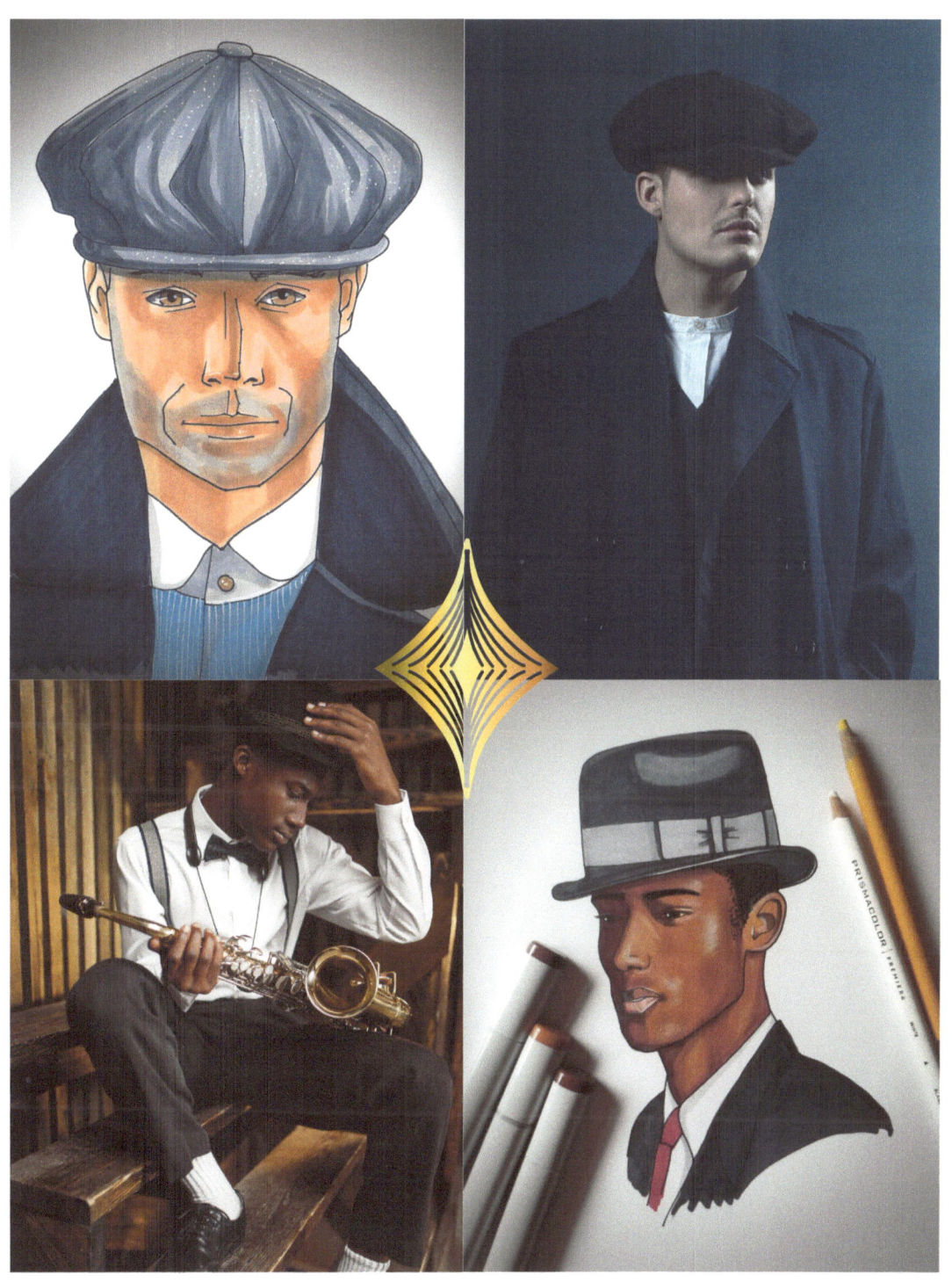

We have done a few gentlemen, so I thought it'd be fun to do an up close shot of a ruffian! And huge thanks to my Facebook Group for the suggestion! Looking for a fun, creative place to show off your drawings? Come join us!
www.facebook.com/groups/awesomeartschool

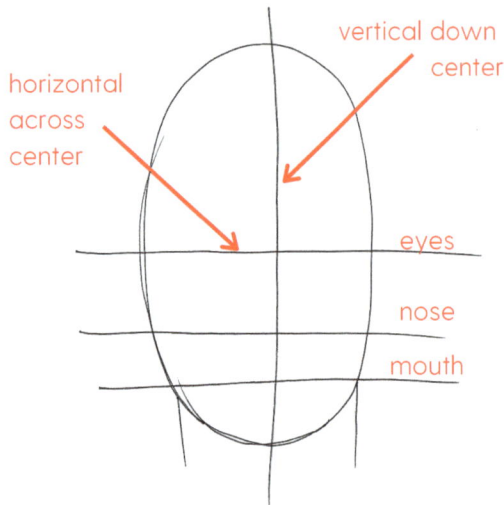

Step 1. Draw an long oval and face guidelines as shown.

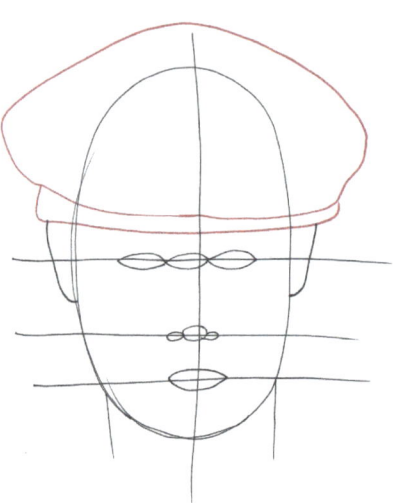

Step 2. Place hat (shown in red) on upper half of oval. Rough in 3 eyes across (for proper spacing) and ovals for the ears, nose and mouth.

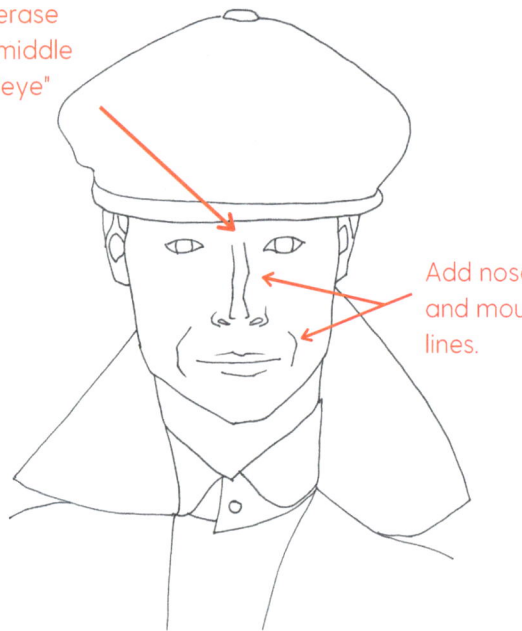

Step 3. Fine tune the facial features. Add coat and shirt outlines.

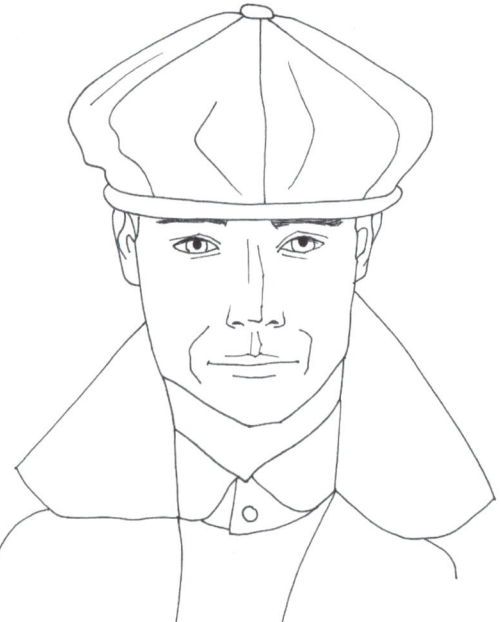

Step 4. Add eyebrows and hat lines.

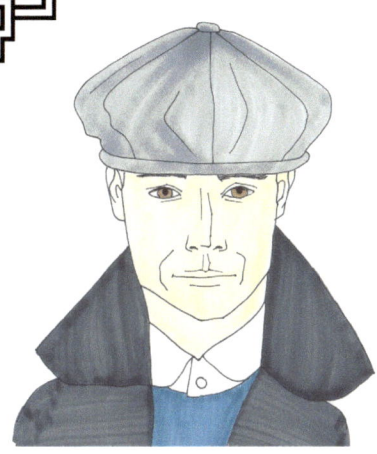

Step 5. Color each part of our ruffian in a light, base color.

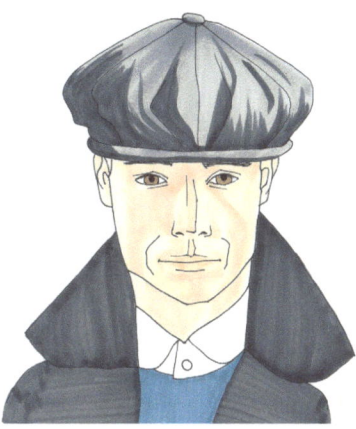

Step 6. Go in to the hat and face with a darker shade.

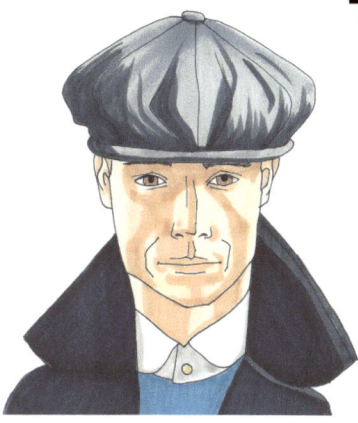

Step 7. Go in to the face and coat and shirt with a even (3rd) darker shade.

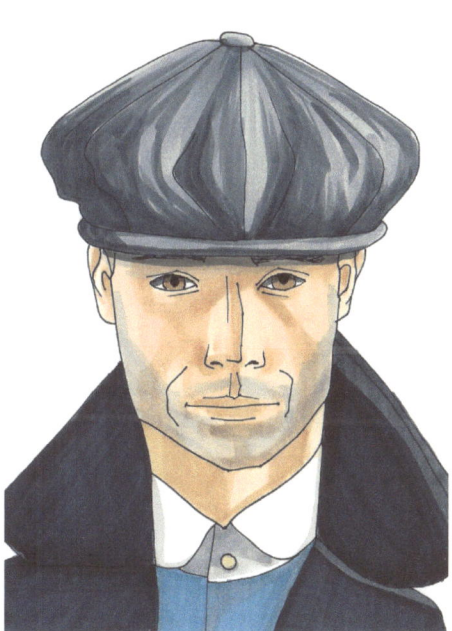

Step 8. Use a light grey to indicate his "scruff". Sweep a medium skin color shade over entire face and neck to blend all previous layers together.

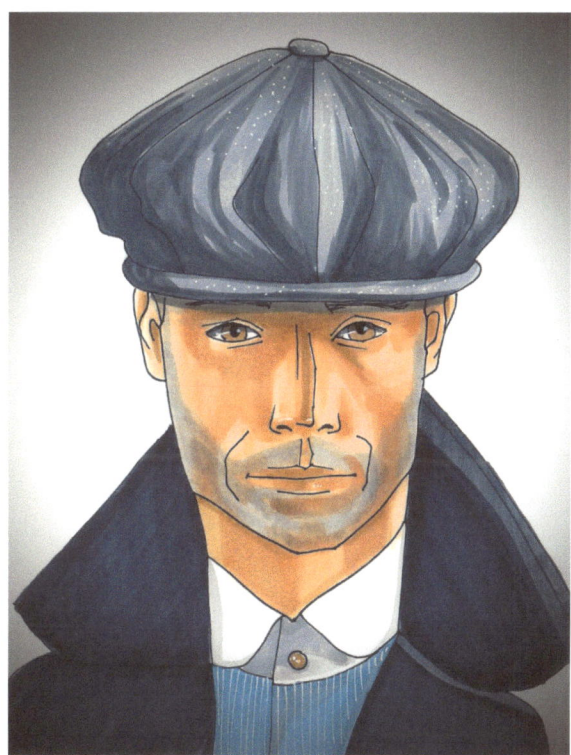

Step 9. Add details to his eyes, hat and shirt with white paint marker! The shadow in this drawing makes him appear even more scruffy! Pretty sure he's a tough guy.

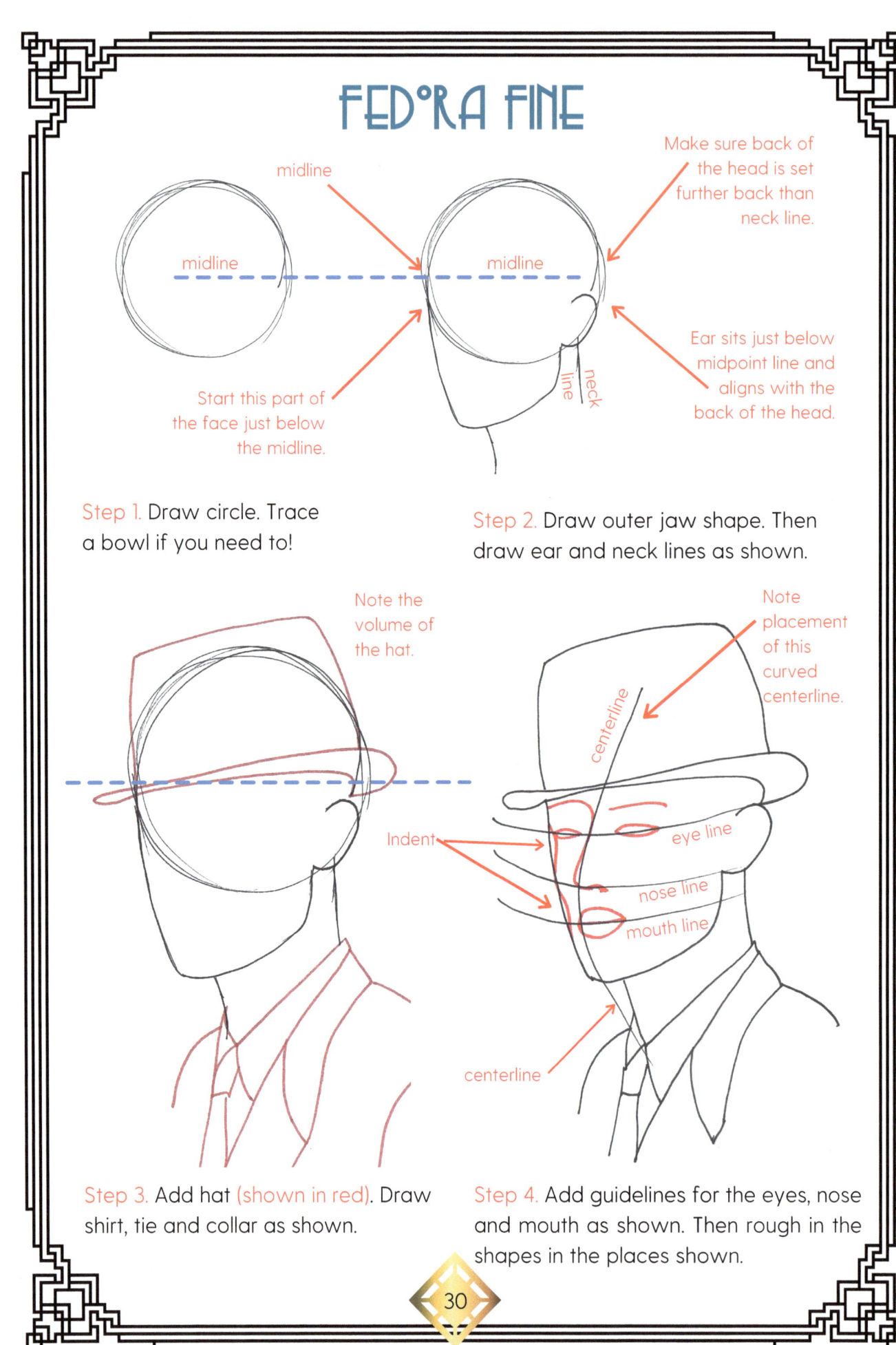

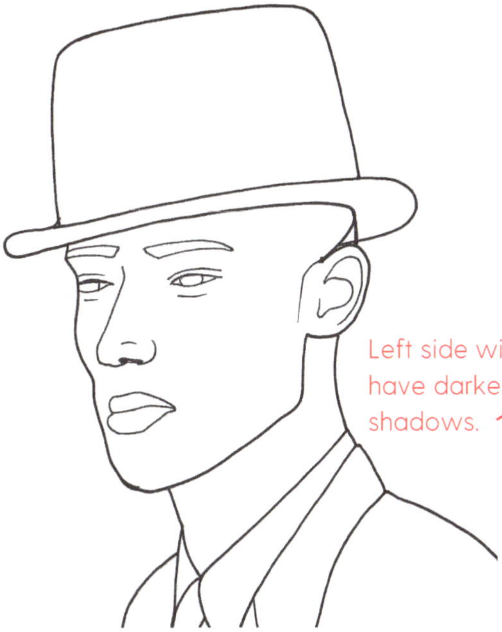

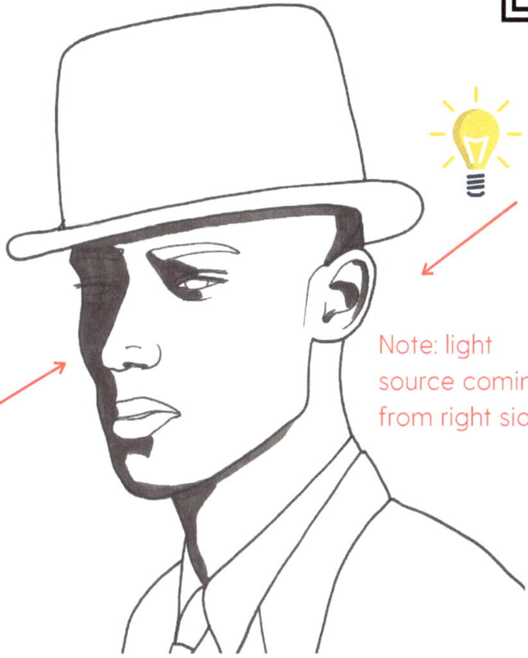

Left side will have darkest shadows.

Note: light source coming from right side.

Step 5. Define the features. Erase the guidelines. Draw outline with fineliner. Collect 3 shades of a skin tone.

Step 6. Apply the darkest of 3 skin shades to the areas shown. I'm using Copic markers here.

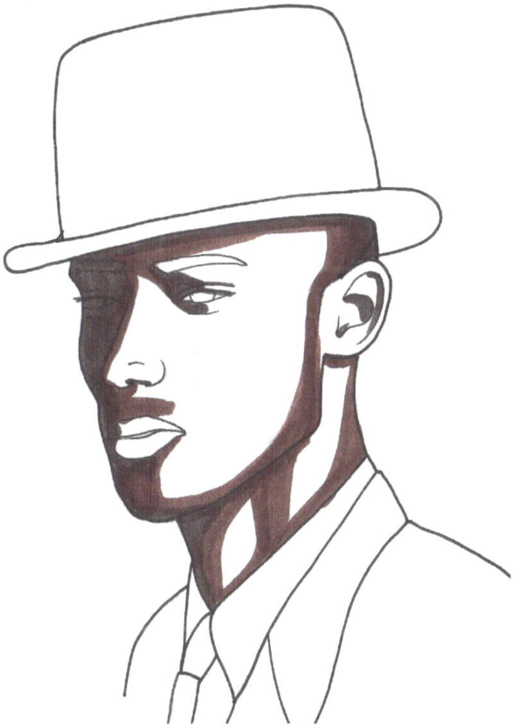

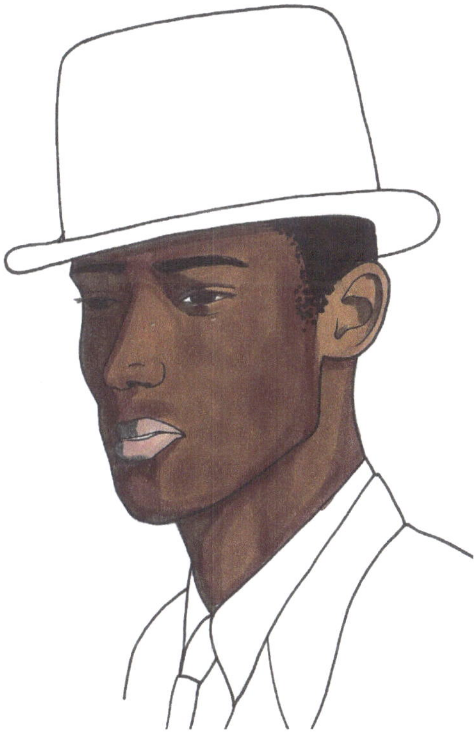

Step 7. Add the middle shade ONLY to areas shown.

Step 8. Add lightest shade to **entire** face (this includes previously colored areas).

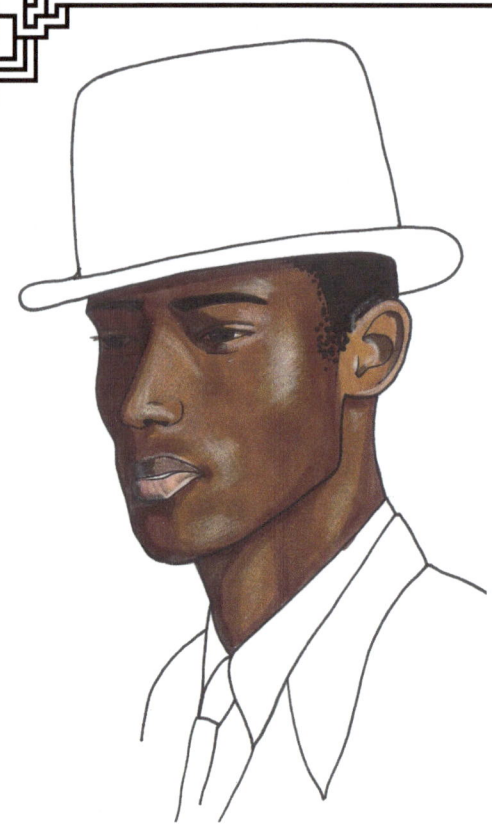

Step 8. Once the markers have been blended (and choosing shades that are close to one another will make blending easier), switch to colored pencils.

With a white pencil, add highlighted areas to the light regions shown (along cheekbone, side of nose and mouth, above the eyebrow, a little bit on the chin, neck and ear).

Then use a yellow shade to help blend the white into the darker brown areas.

Step 9. Color the hat and clothes as you see fit! Use grey on the white shirt to give it a 3 dimensional appearance.

Step 10. Color the lips in with dark pinks and add a white highlight to each pupil so that you can see the twinkle of the eye, even through the dark shadow. Well done!!

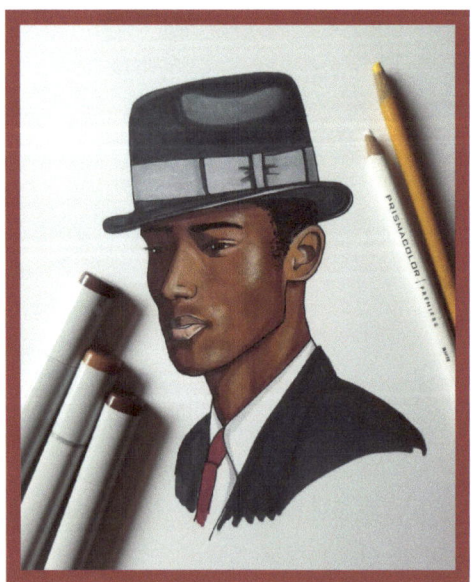

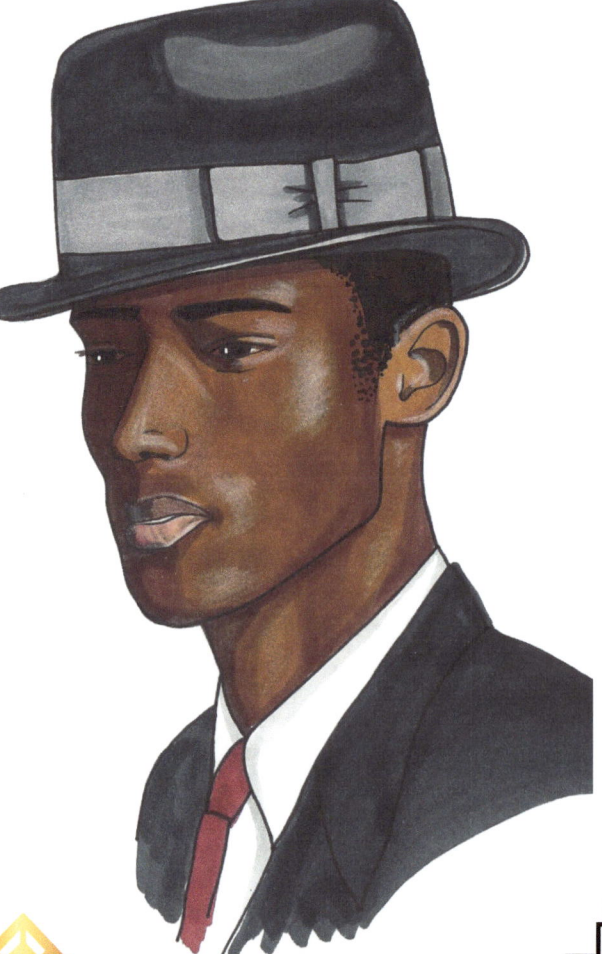

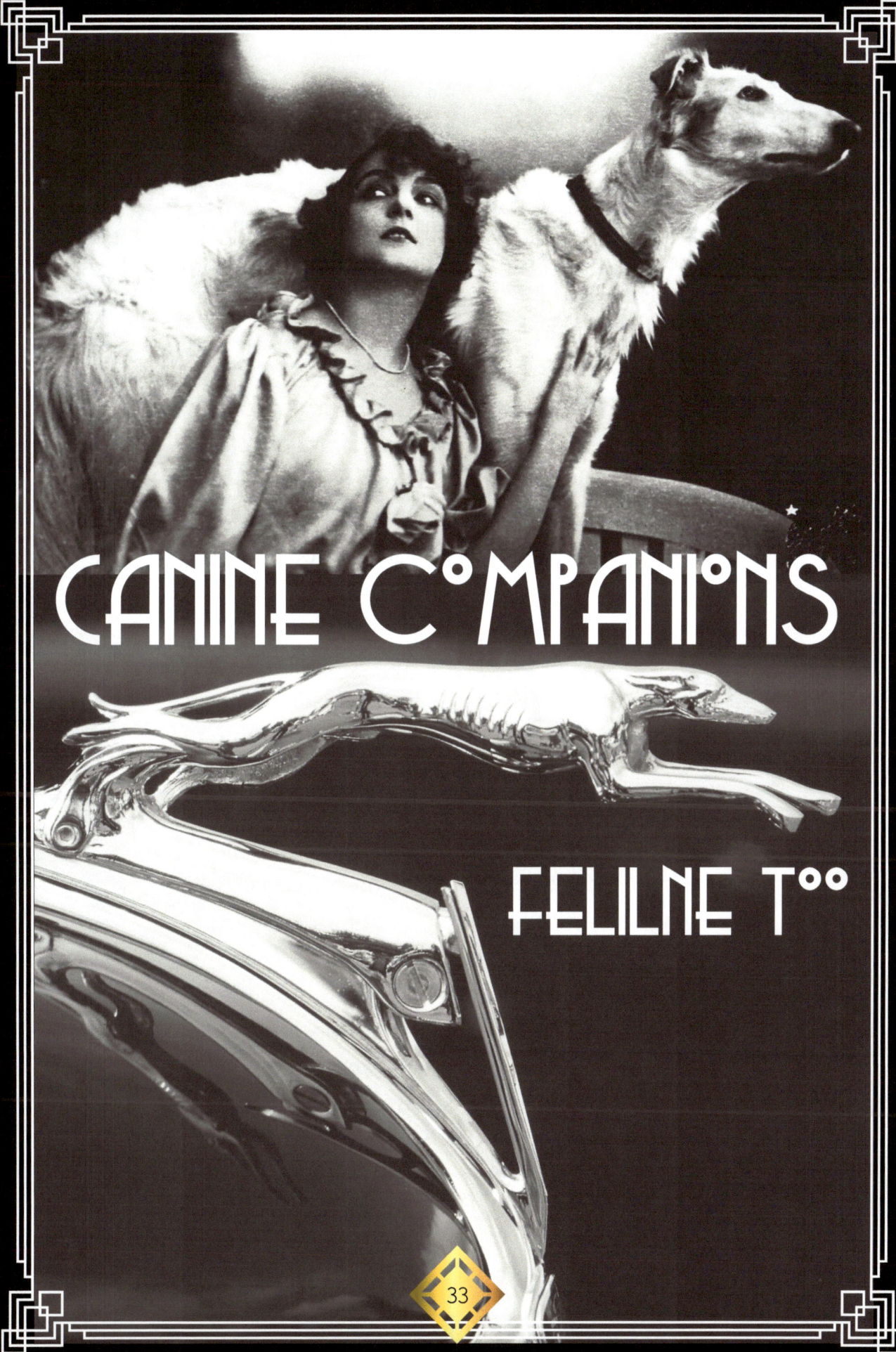

One wouldn't naturally suppose that there'd be a dog of an era. When it came to Art Deco, there absolutely was! There were a few, in fact!

It turns out that the sleek designs of the decor and fashion of the day were often reflected in their canine and feline friends!

Greyhounds, Borzois, Standard Poodles and Great Danes were on the top of the popularity list followed closely by the Saluki (another influence of an Egyptian discovery), French and English Bulldog, Daschund, Pekinese and Scottie! We will draw them all and more!

Drawing dogs can be easy or very complicated, depending on the breed you're trying to depict and the position of the dog.

In the following pages, I will recommend a number of different ways to do the drawings. No matter which approach I mention, I will always be showing you the easiest way!

The Great Dane

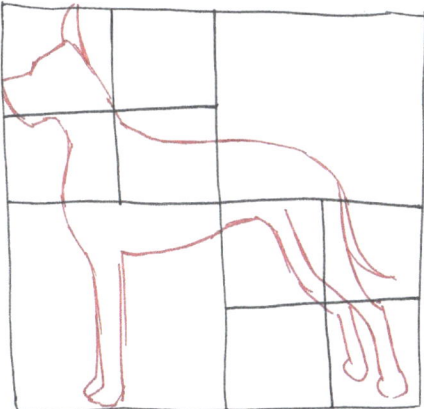

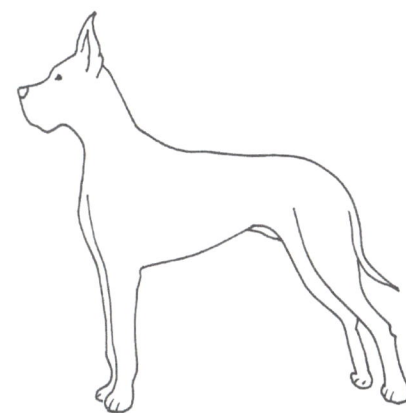

Step 1. Use as many (or as few) Quadrants as you need to be able to draw all the body parts.

Step 2. Use this outline, together with the **Quadrant** method, to sketch the dog.

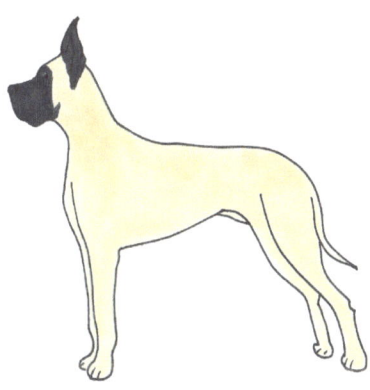

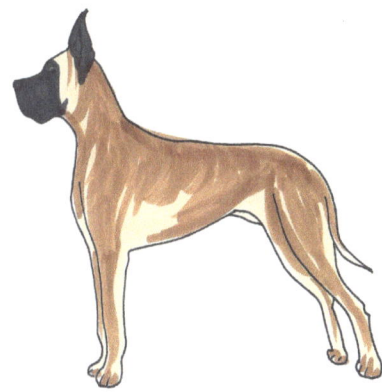

Step 3. Color the face and ears black. Color the body a light sand color.

Step 4. Use a darker color to create darker areas of fur.

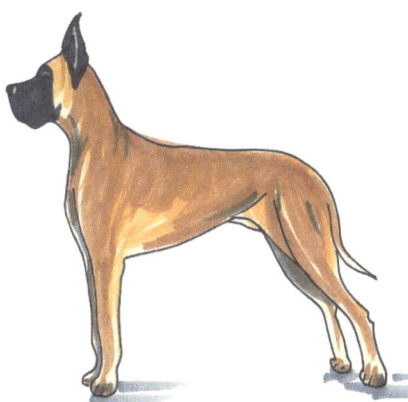

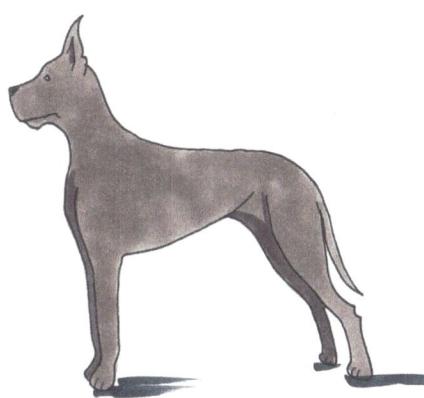

Step 5. Use a mid tone color to tie the 2 colors together.

Great Dane coats come in a beautifully variety of colors!

SALUKI

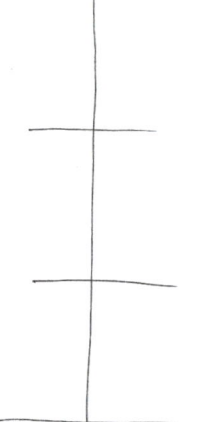

Step 1. Establish a height for your dog. Divide into 3 equal sections (roughly).

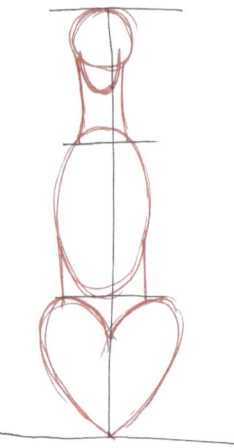

Step 2. Sketch in the shapes as shown (in red).

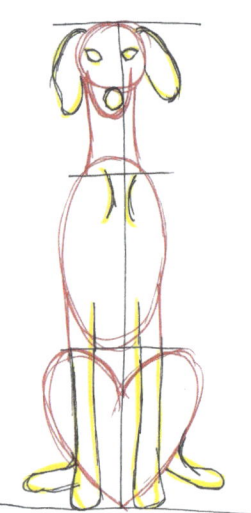

Step 3. Add legs, chest lines, paws and ears! (Shown in yellow).

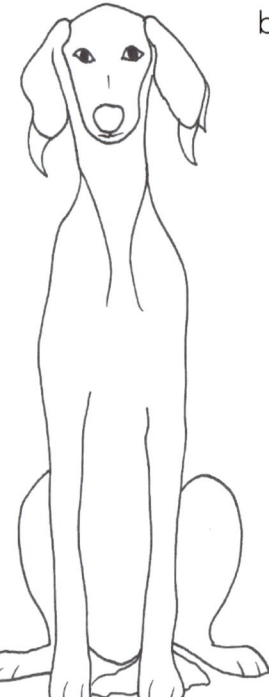

Step 4. Finalize outline. Erase guidelines.

Salukis can be sandy, white or black! Don't forget to use your white gel pen for the eye!

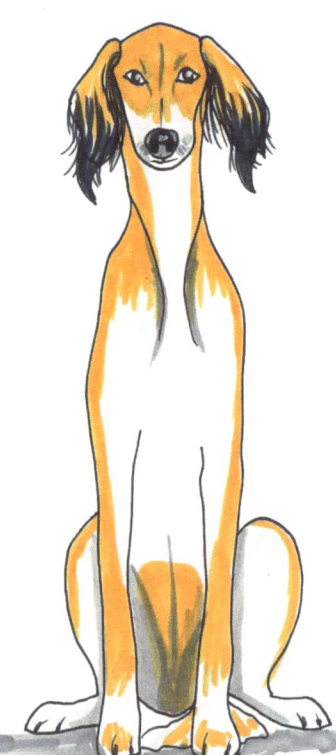

Step 5. Color with your favorite markers, paint or pencils!

SCOTTIE

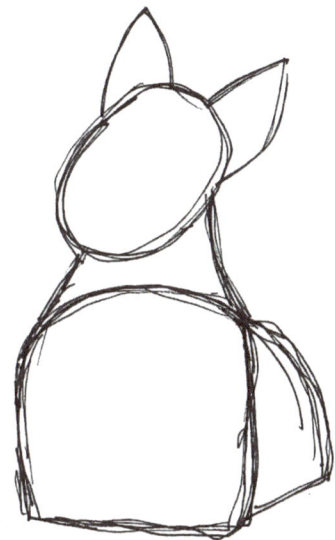

Step 1. Scotties are fun little guys to draw! First block in the simple shapes, like this.

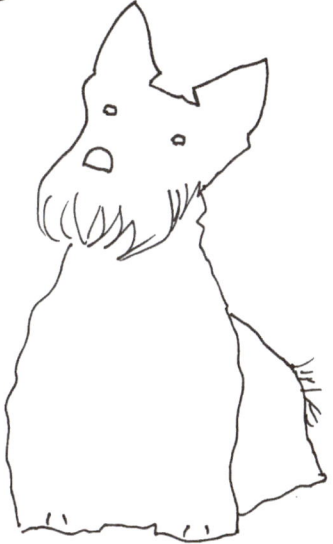

Step 2. Now refine the outline a bit more and erase your original guidelines.

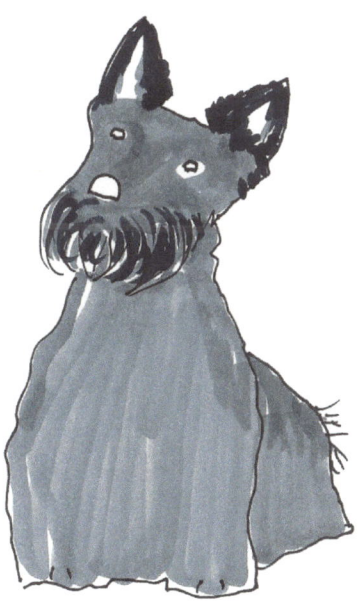

Step 3. Begin coloring by laying down an initial shade of medium to dark grey.

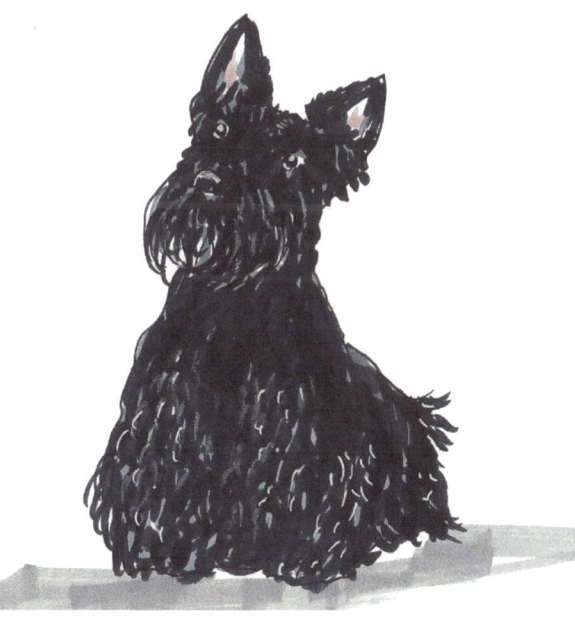

Step 4. Then add short, individual strokes of black. You can add highlights to the eyes, nose and hairs with a white gel pen if you like!

French Bulldog Puppy

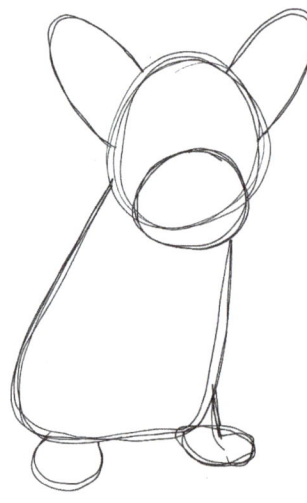

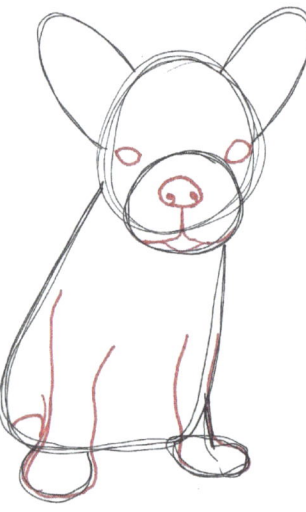

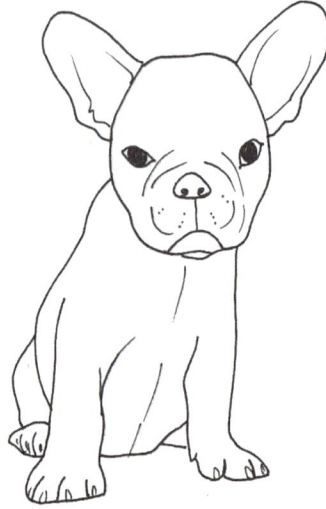

Step 1. First draw these generalized shapes.

Step 2. Add the nose, eyes and leg lines.

Step 3. Refine the outline and add details shown.

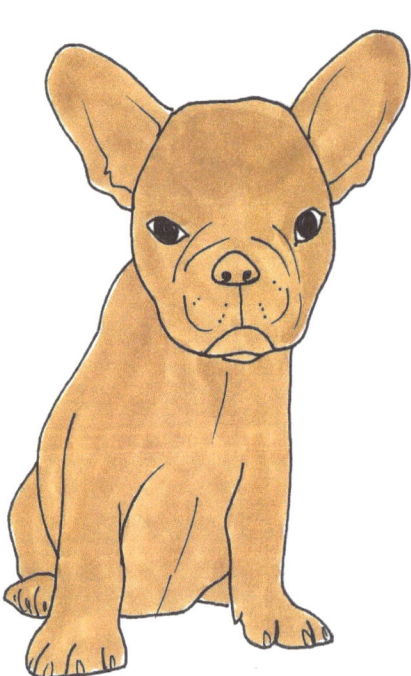

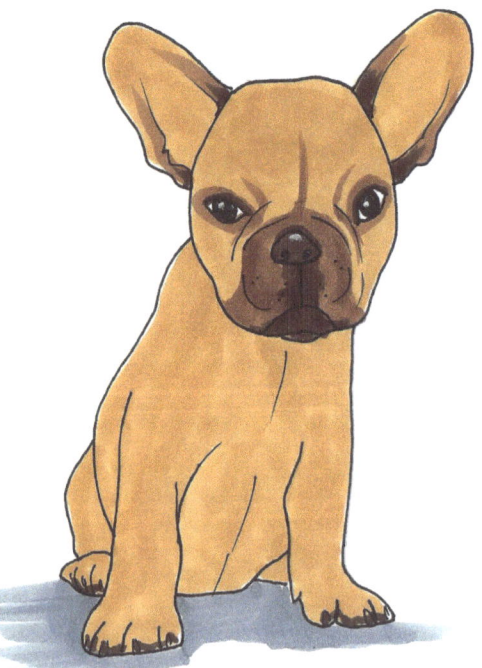

Step 4. Start with a solid layer of color. French Bulldogs also come in an adorable range of colors!

Step 5. Add darker areas to the face, ears and toes! Look at photo references for other coat color ideas!

Standard Poodle

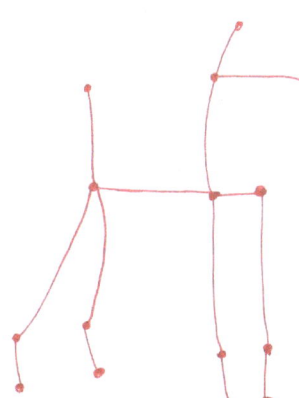

Step 1. Start with a wire-frame this time. Then we will build up from there!

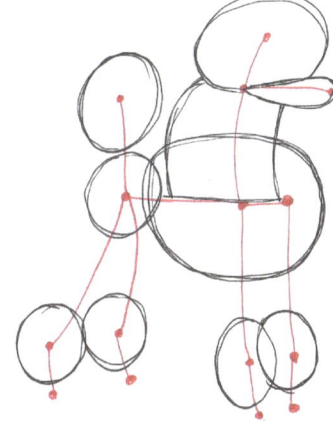

Step 2. Add the big ovals and circles around the red dots as shown.

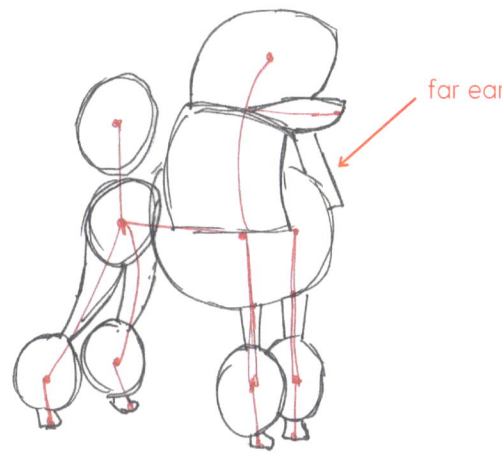

far ear

Step 3. Add leg outlines and far ear.

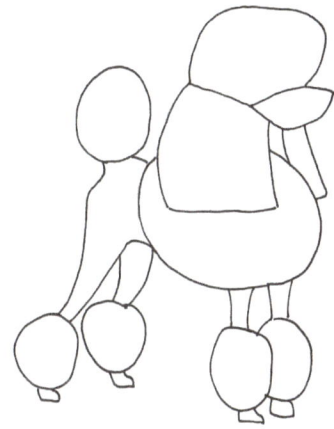

Step 4. Erase guidelines. Outline with fineliner.

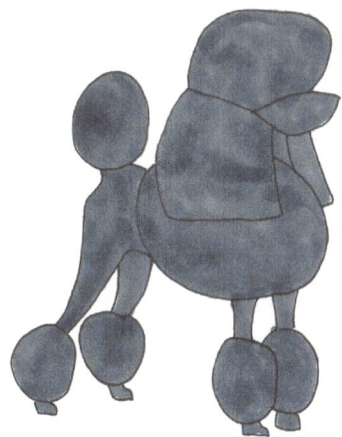

Step 5. Use one base color.

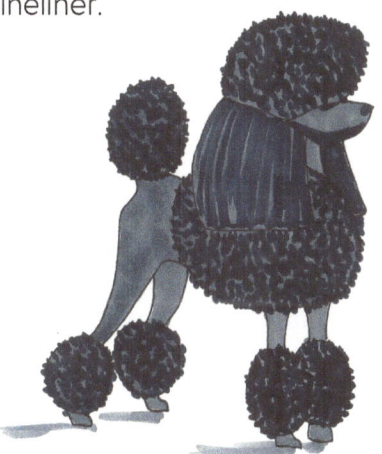

Step 6. Stipple the furball areas in a darker shade. So fun!

Pekinese

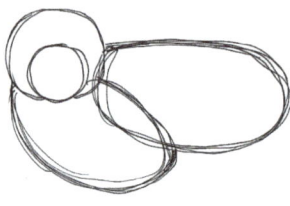
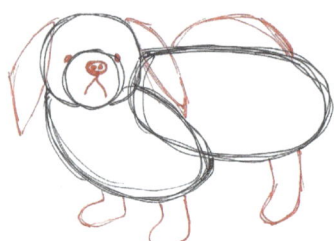
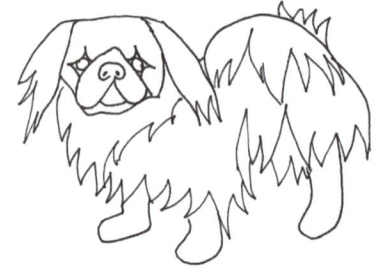

Step 1. Draw 2 circles for the face. Draw 2 ovals for the body.

Step 2. Add ears, the face, legs and tail (shown in red).

Step 3. Go around the body guidelines with shaggy hair shapes in pencil.

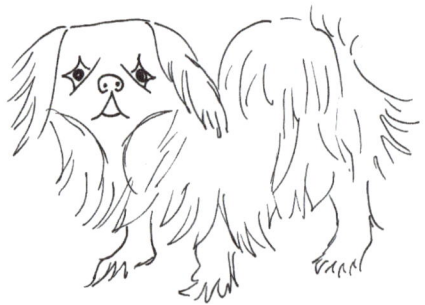
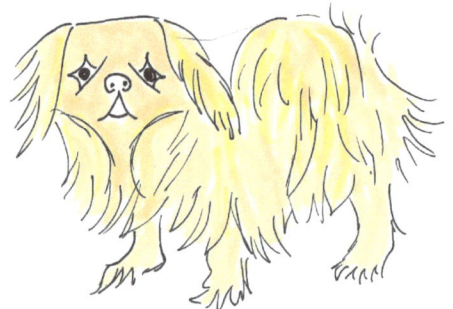

Step 4. Either refine your pencil lines by erasing, or redraw a more delicate version of hair.

Step 5. Color entire body with a light fur color.

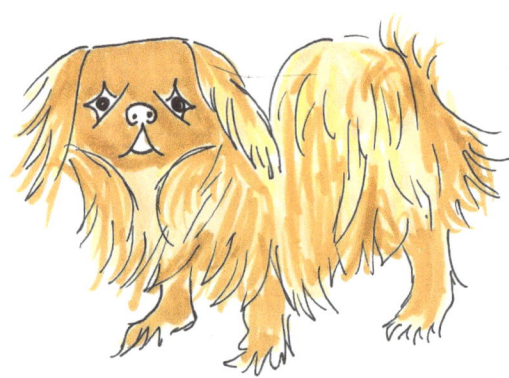
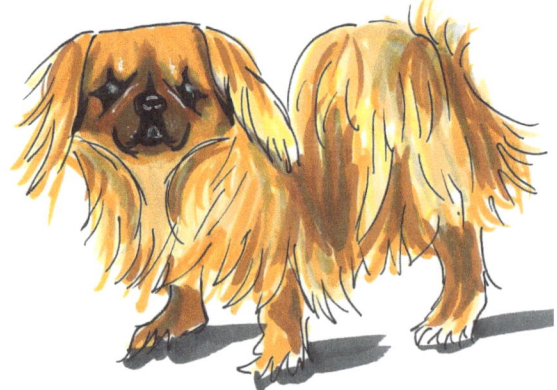

Step 6. Add in a second, darker color. Intersperse it amongst the light color. Make face the darkest.

Step 7. Use a third, dark color on face, on legs and scattered throughout. Use black to define the eyes and adorable snout!

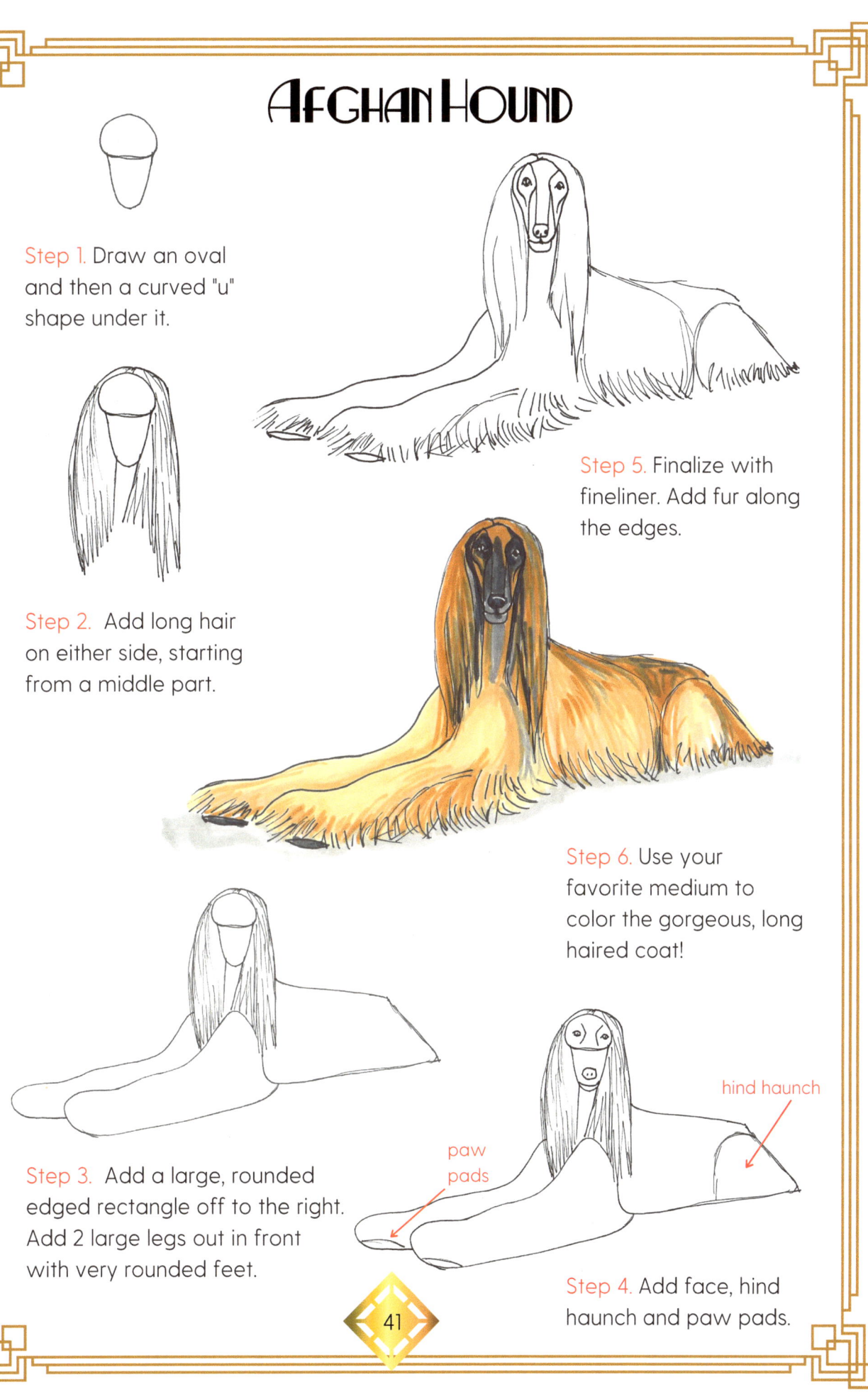

Wire Fox Terrier

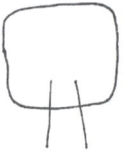
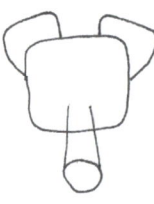
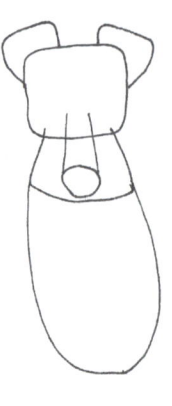
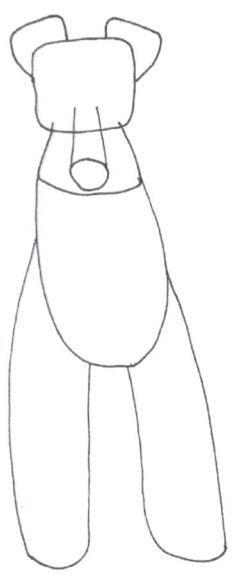

Step 1. Draw a rounded square with 2 lines coming out of it.

Step 2. Add soft square shapes coming off the top. Add a circle at the bottom.

Step 3. Add elongated shape with a line partway through.

Step 4. Add broad, rounded leg shapes.

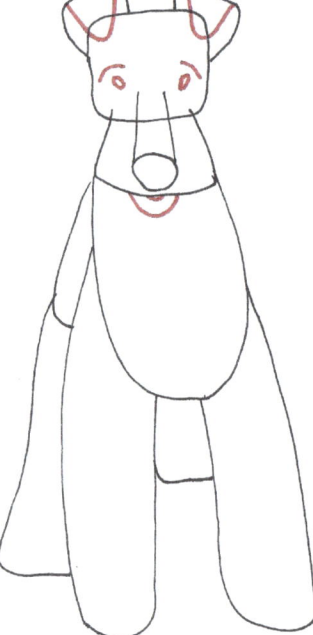
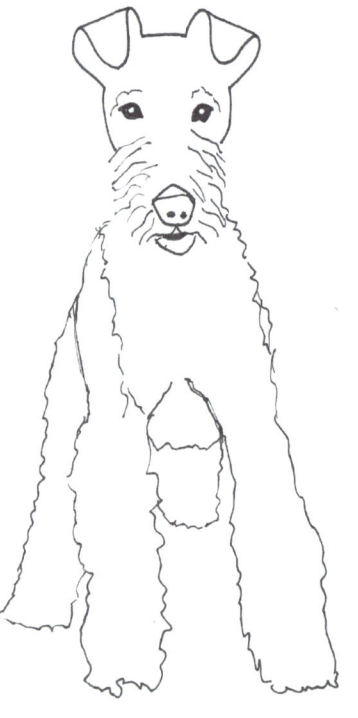
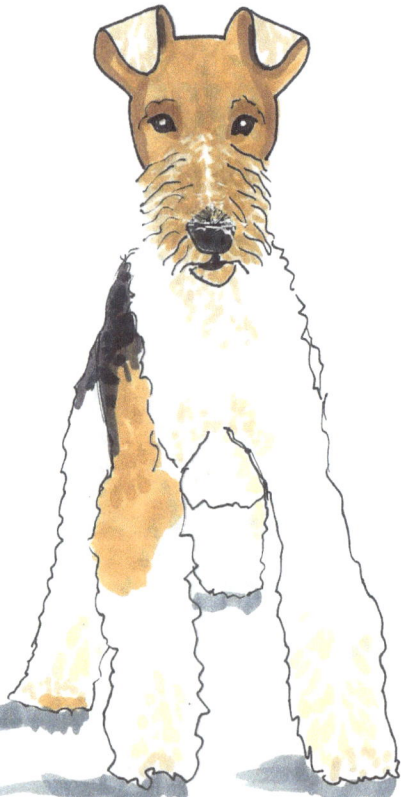

Step 5. Add the ear flaps (triangles shown above in red), eyes, lip and rear legs.

Step 6. Redraw in your favorite fineliner. Make outlines scraggly to help give the illusion of fur.

Step 7. Color with your favorite medium!

Art Deco Cats

The excavation of King Tut's tomb in 1922 had a rippling effect on many facets of culture in the Art Deco period. Such influences include the wearing of Kohl eye make up, bangle bracelets and....a heightened adoration of cats! Without a doubt, the Siamese and the black cat are the most iconic of this time period and we will learn to draw both!

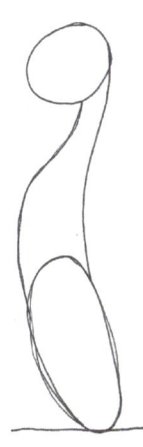

Step 1. Begin with 2 ovals connected by 2 curved lines.

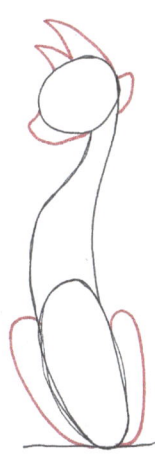

Step 2. Add curved triangles for the ears. Add the 4 curved lines (in red).

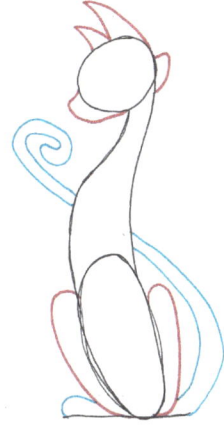

Step 3. Draw a long, curved tail. Add front paw (shown in blue).

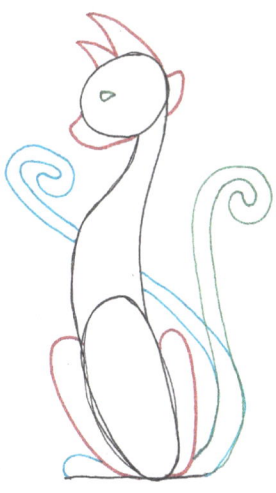

Step 4. Add a small eye. Now is a great time to see how other tails would look!

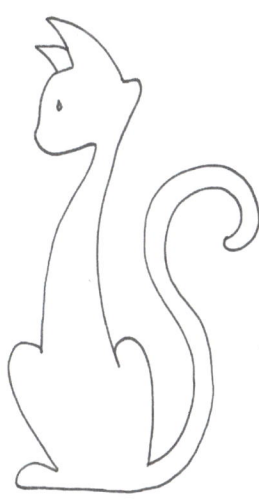

Step 5. Finalize your outline with a fineliner.

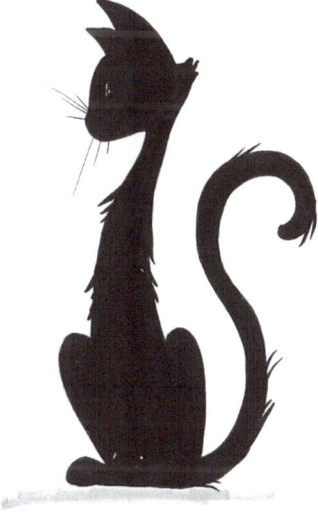

Step 6. Color solid black. Add little tuffs off hair. Add fine whiskers! So cute!

Siamese

Long, lean and lanky are these cool cats! And so fun to draw too!

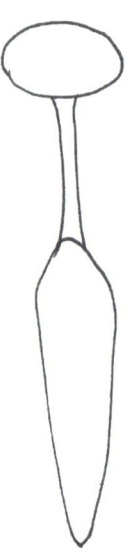

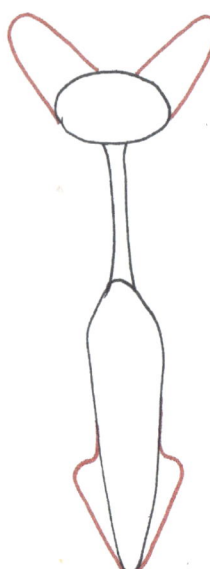

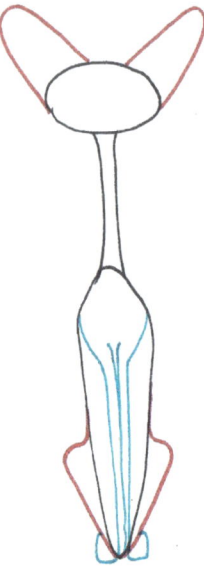

Step 1. Draw an oval for the head. Connect it to an elongated shape at the bottom.

Step 2. Add ears and hind haunches (in red).

Step 3. Add front legs and paws (blue).

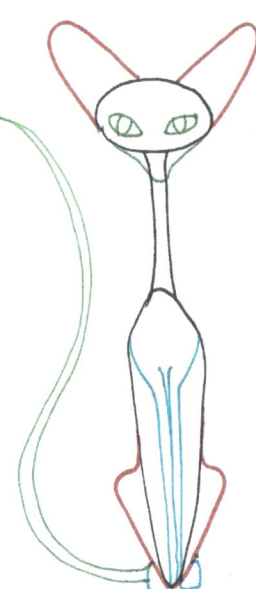

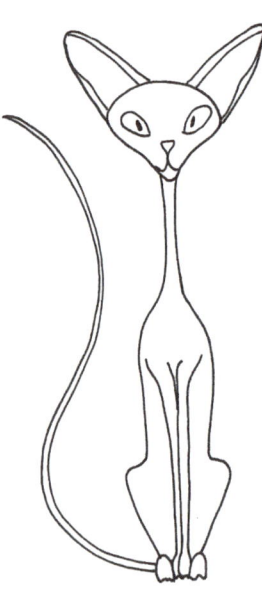

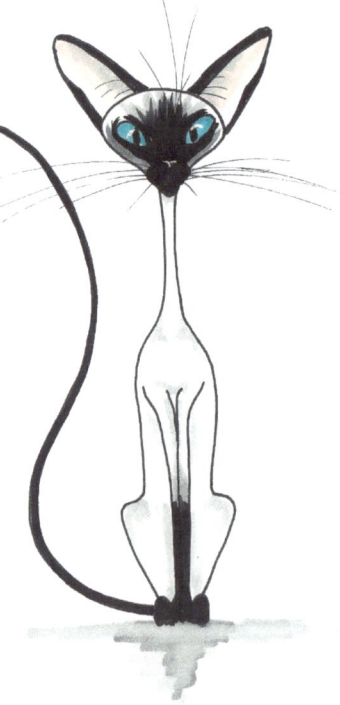

Step 4. Add eyes and tail (in green).

Step 5. Finalize your outline with a fineliner.

Step 6. Color according to your favorite Siamese breed!

Persian

There isn't a more glamorous cat than the Persian, so it's only too appropriate that we draw one here (and I KNOW the flappers in Vol. 1 would love one!).

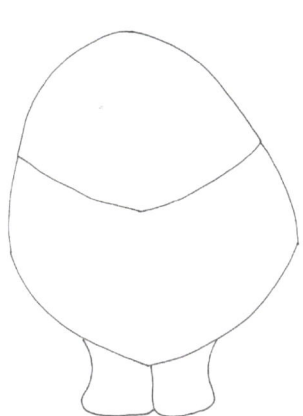 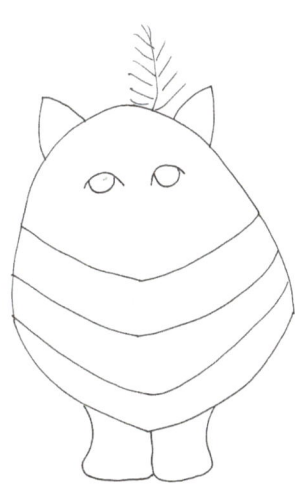 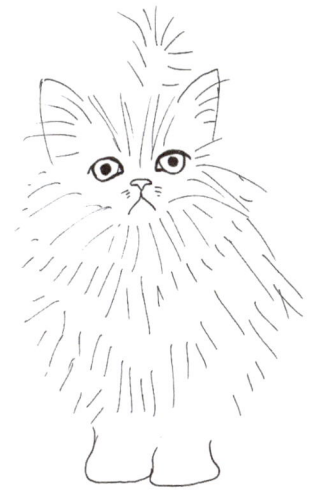

Step 1. Draw a bulky egg shape with line across the middle. Add wide legs at bottom.

Step 2. Add ears, eyes, tail and 2 more lines.

Step 3. In place of lines, sketch loose fur lines. Add pupils, nose and mouth.

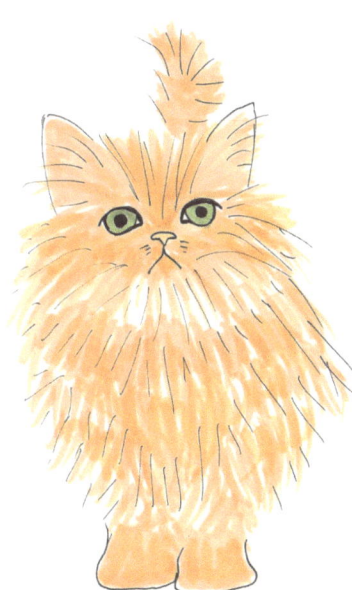 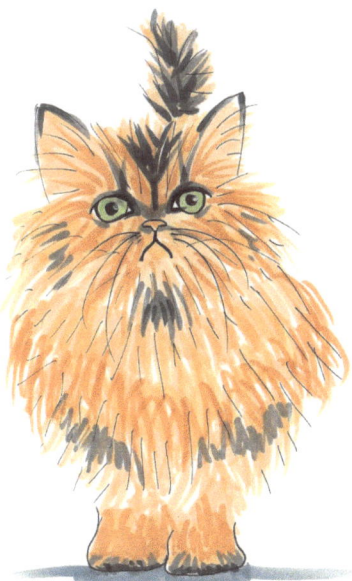 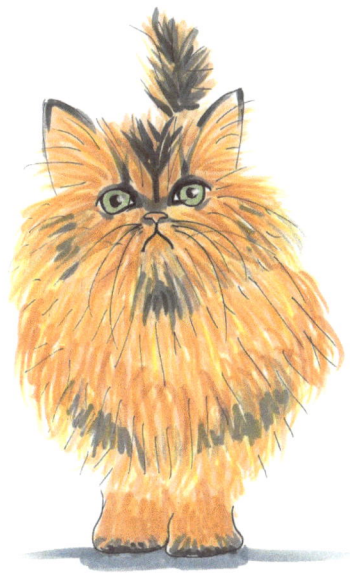

Step 4. Add lots and lots of individual lines for the fluffy fur using just one or two colors.

Step 5. Add some dark markings. Add whiskers!

Step 6. Add some colored pencils over marker to make her even fluffier!

Inspiration!

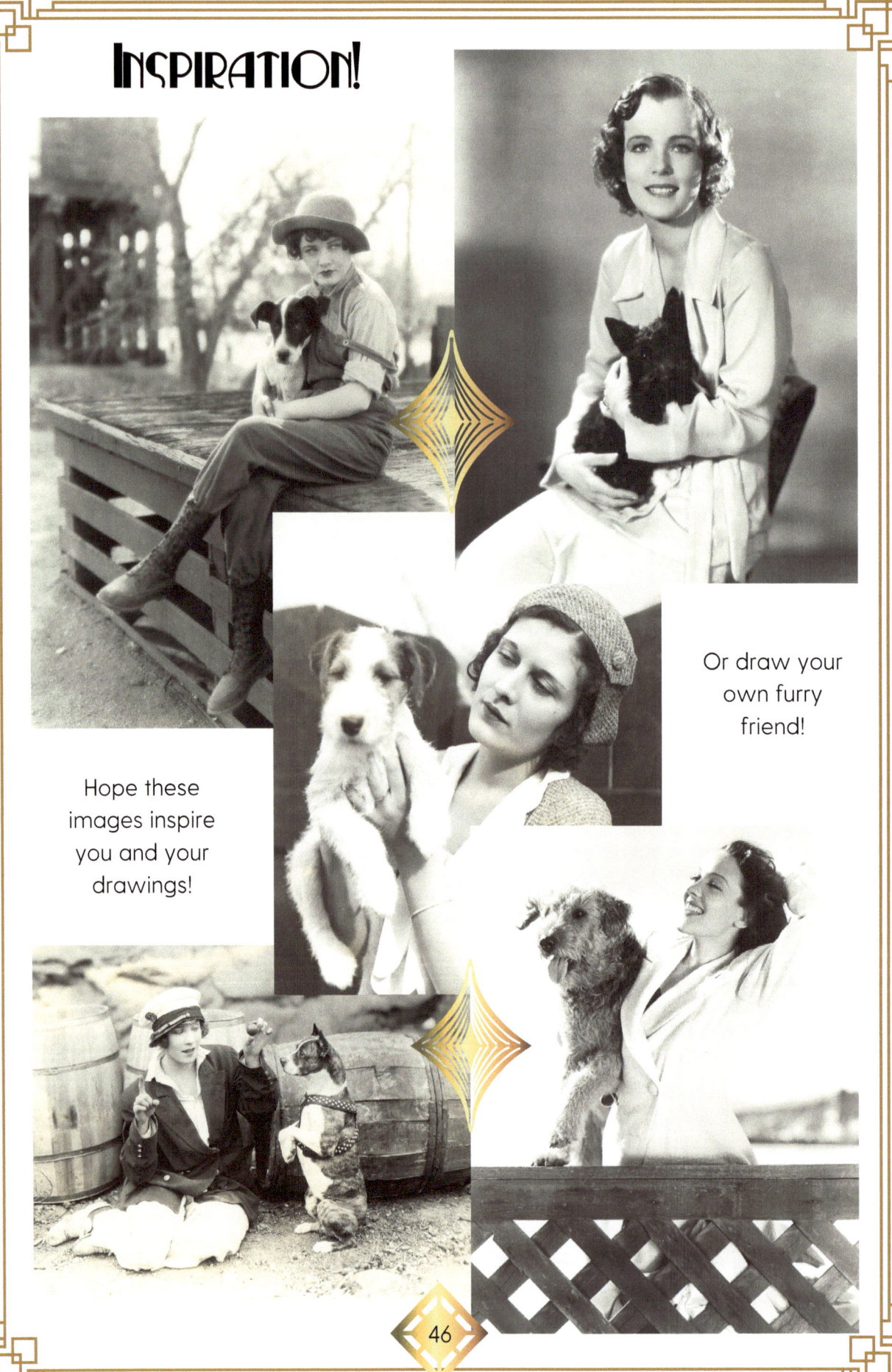

Or draw your own furry friend!

Hope these images inspire you and your drawings!

FURNISHINGS

The Art Deco period, in terms of furniture and design, was born at the Exposition des Arts Decoratif et Industriels Modernes held in Paris in 1925.

20 countries participated and over 15 million people attended this six month event.

The most unique attribute of this event (and ultimately, why the United States was left out of it), was that no design could be based upon the designs of the past.

Each design of furniture, clothing, and architecture, had to be completely new (hence "Moderne") and so Art Deco was born.

Drawing furniture is a lovely break from drawing complicated faces and figures, but that doesn't mean it isn't fun!

The rich, bold colors and velvety, soft upholstery are easy to draw and look fabulous when colored in using a myriad of mediums! For most of the drawings, I used Fountain Pen Ink to color. See the link to the videos for more info on this intriguing medium that's so fun to paint with!

UPHOLSTERED FURNITURE

Art Deco chairs came in rich colors, geometric shapes and were as comfortable as they were stylish! Their simplicity makes them fun and easy to draw and their bold colors inspire me to use my watercolors and inks!

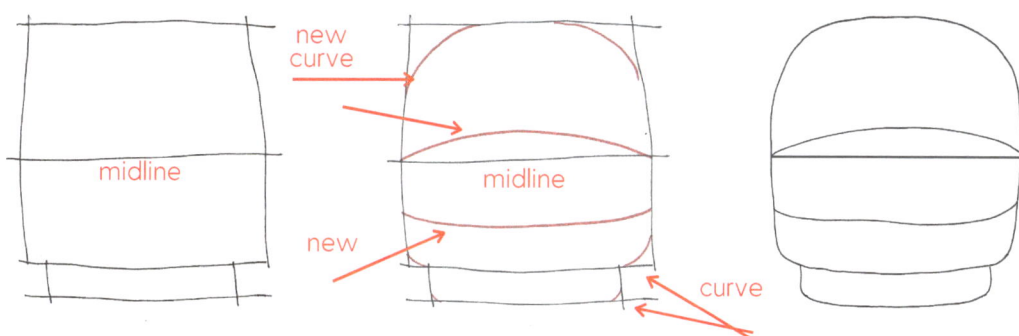

Step 1. Draw a square. Draw a line through the middle. Draw a small rectangle at the bottom.

Step 2. Curve all corners. Add a curved line just above the midline. Add another line in the lower section.

Step 3. Outline final shape in fineliner and erase your guidelines.

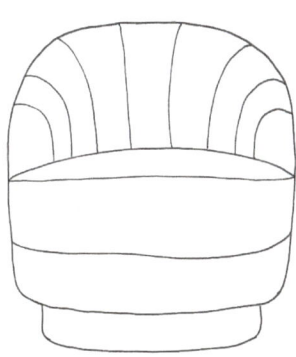

Step 4. Draw 8 curved lines coming out of seat cushion.

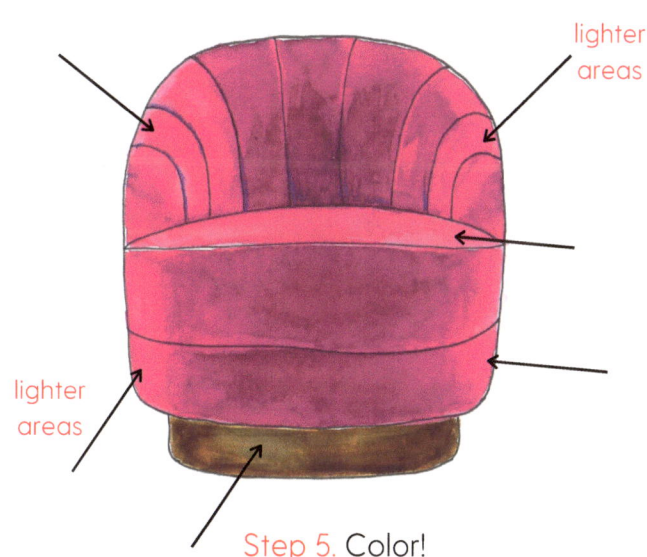

Step 5. Color!

I colored this chair using only fountain pen inks by Noodlers in the color Saguaro Wine. To create the lighter areas shown (that help create the illusion of depth), simply wet those areas with plain water and a damp brush, and "lift" the color off by blotting with a dry paper towel. Magic!

49

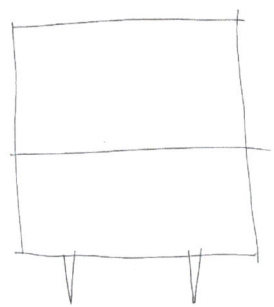 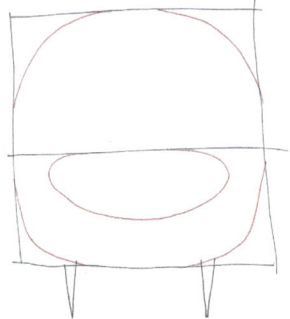 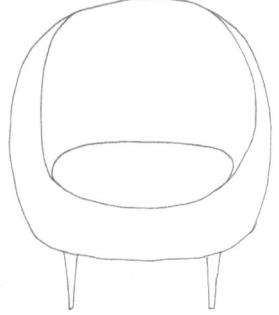

Step 1. Draw a box. Draw a line across the middle. Add triangular feet.

Step 2. Curve corners. Draw an oval at center line.

Step 3. Finalize lines. Draw curves up sides.

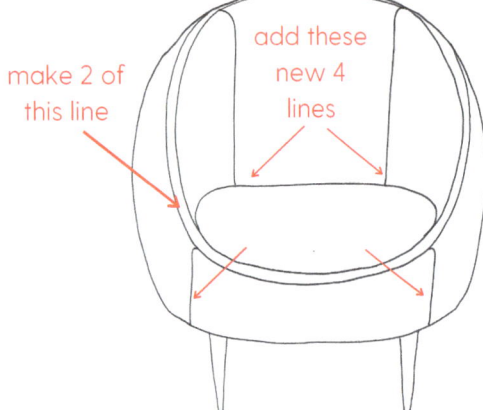 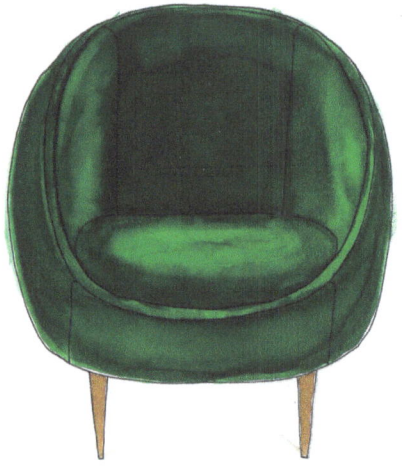

Step 4. Double sweeping curve line. Add 4 vertical lines.

Step 5. Color in with the medium of your choice! This is Cactus Green by Noodler's Ink.

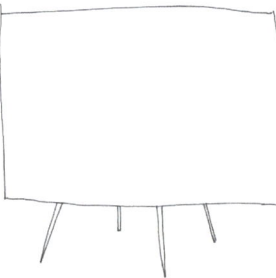 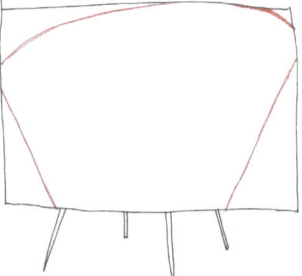 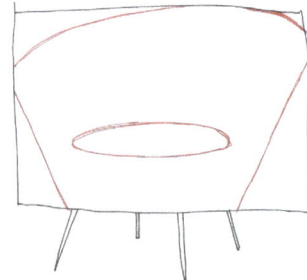

Step 1. This next one is my favorite! Begin by drawing a rectangle and 4 feet. Each spread out and a different length.

Step 2. Add 2 curved lines at the top. Add 2 straight, diagonal lines for the sides.

Step 3. Add a narrow oval for seat.

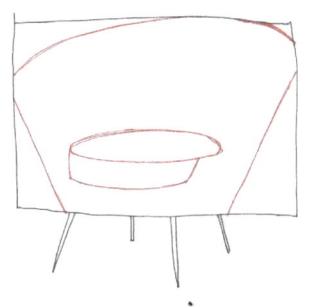
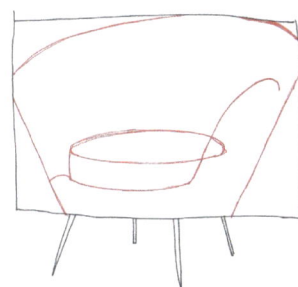
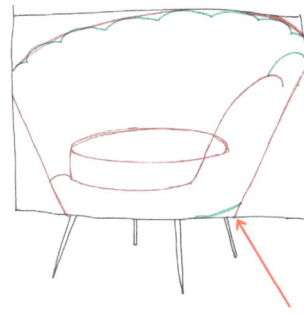

Step 4. Draw a rectangle off of the oval.

Step 5. Draw 2 curved lines as shown.

Step 6. Add scallops at top and a curved line at bottom (in green).

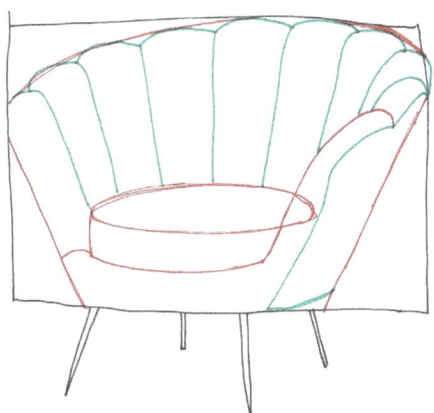
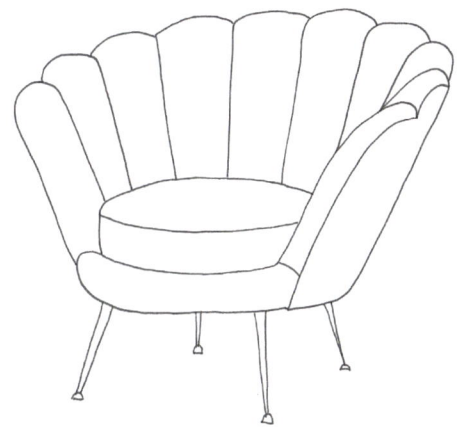

Step 7. Connect scallops with straight lines that end at seat cushion (oval).

Step 8. Erase guidelines and outline!

 Watch how to render these chairs in BOTH watercolors (left) and ink (right). https://bit.ly/artdecochairs

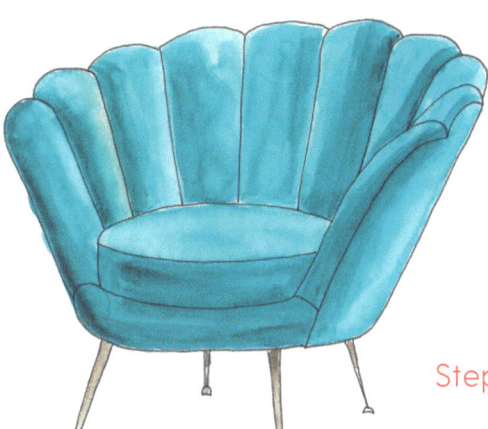
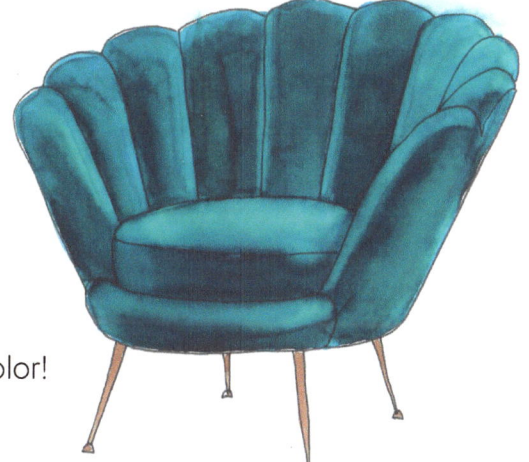

Step 9. Color!

Painted with Daniel Smith Watercolor (pthalo blue)

Painted with Noodler's Ink in Turquoise

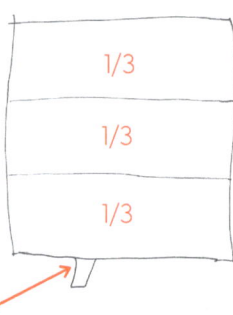

Step 1. Draw a rectangle. Divide into 3rds. Draw a foot.

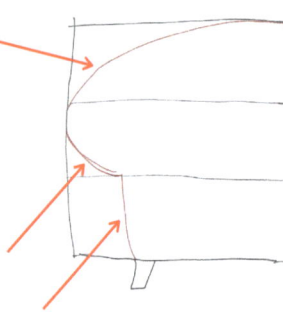

Step 2. Draw 3 lines lines Use guidelines to help!

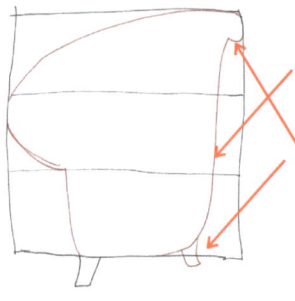

Step 3. Add 1 small curve. 1 long vertical and 1 foot.

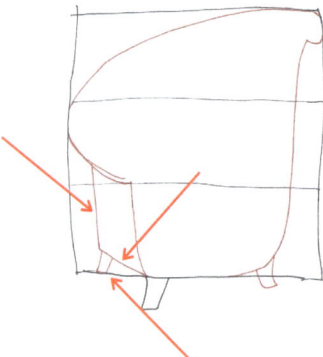

Step 4. Draw 2 straight lines and 1 foot.

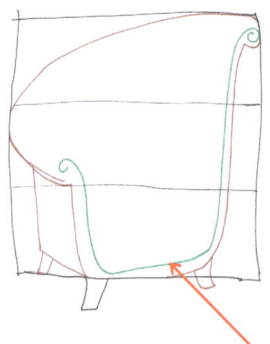

Step 5. Add swirls and inner line (in green).

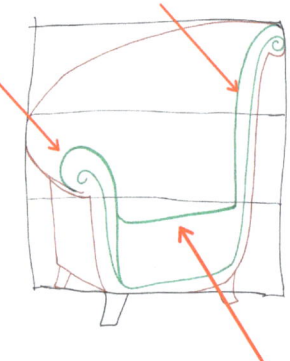

Step 6. Add 3 more lines (in green) to form seat and arms of chair.

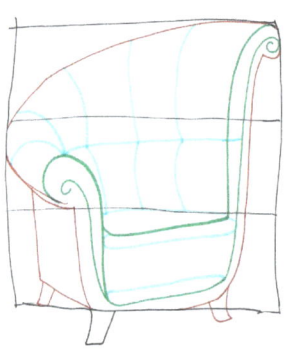

Step 7. Add cushion lines (in blue).

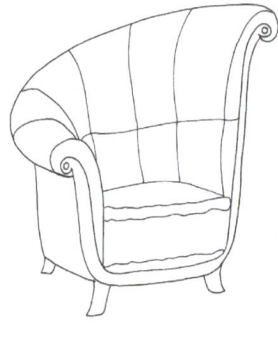

Step 8. Outline in fineliner and erase guidelines.

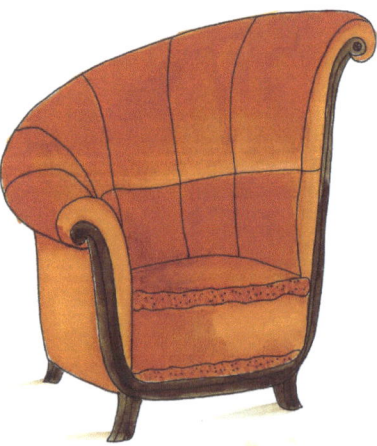

Step 9. Color!

Painted with Noodler's Ink in Habanera

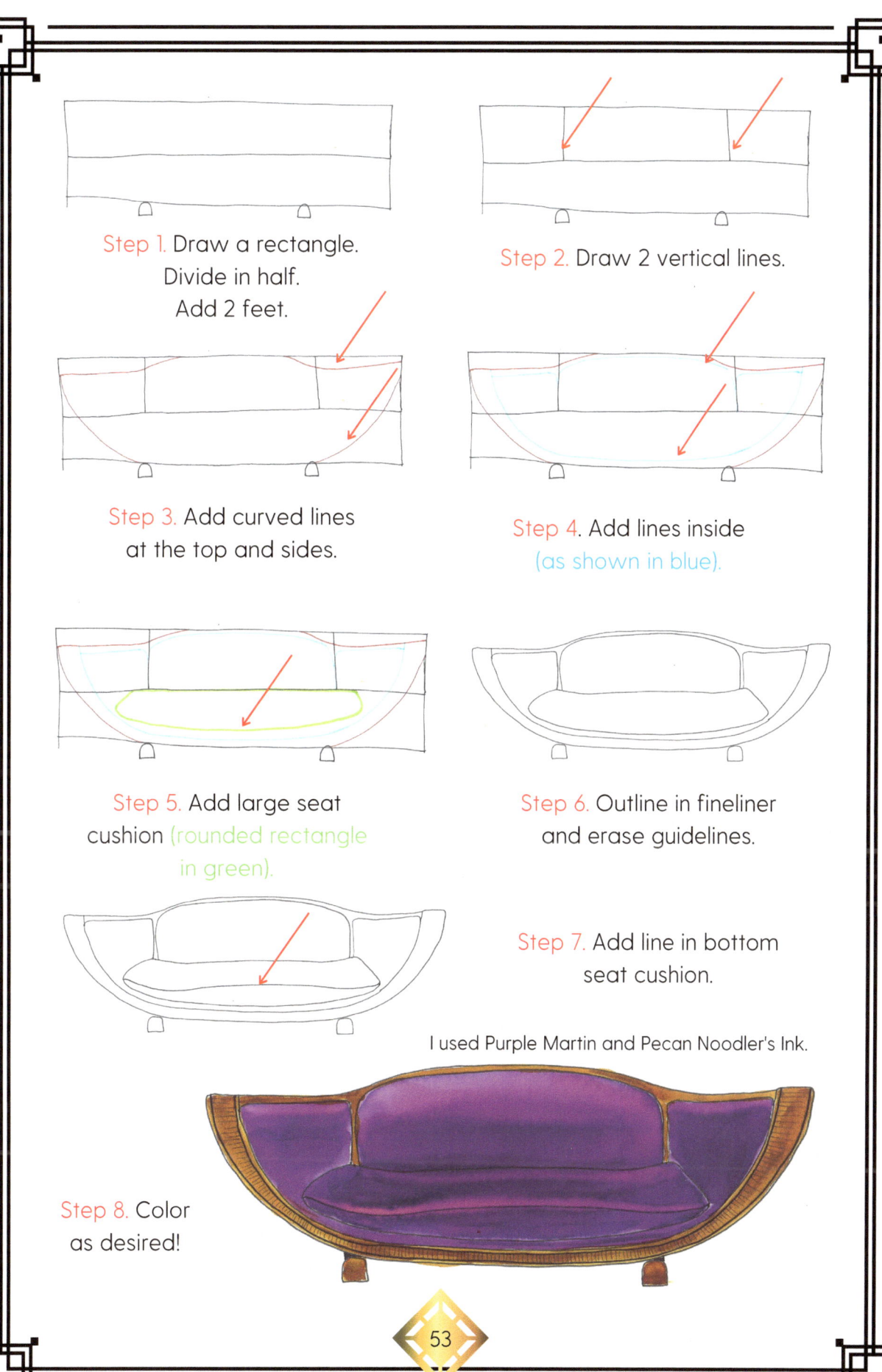

Step 1. Draw a rectangle. Divide in half. Add 2 feet.

Step 2. Draw 2 vertical lines.

Step 3. Add curved lines at the top and sides.

Step 4. Add lines inside (as shown in blue).

Step 5. Add large seat cushion (rounded rectangle in green).

Step 6. Outline in fineliner and erase guidelines.

Step 7. Add line in bottom seat cushion.

I used Purple Martin and Pecan Noodler's Ink.

Step 8. Color as desired!

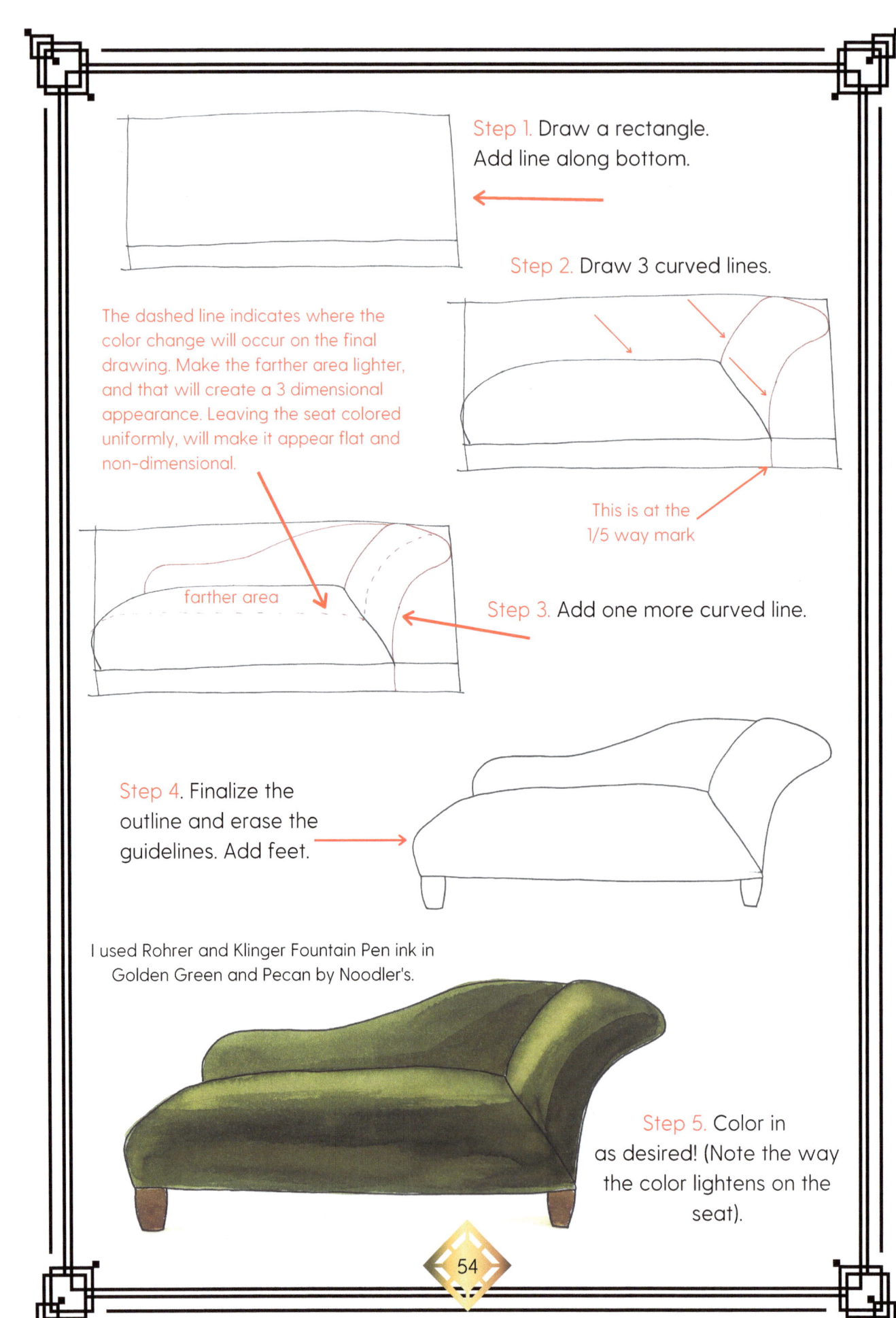

BEDROOM COMFORT

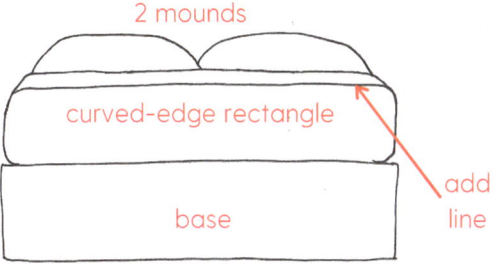

Step 1. Draw a rectangular base. Then add a curve-edged rectangle on top. Add horizontal line and 2 mounds.

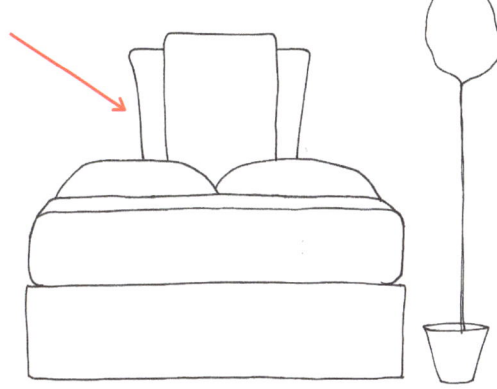

Step 2. Draw 3 rectangles above mounds. Add basic plant pot and single large leaf.

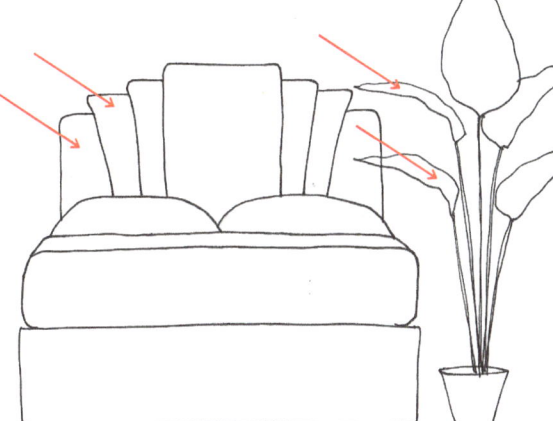

Step 3. Finish headboard by drawing 2 more rectangles on each side. Add 4 more leaves to the potted plant so it's somewhat symmetrical.

Turn the pages to learn how to draw the rest of these fun, fab pieces!

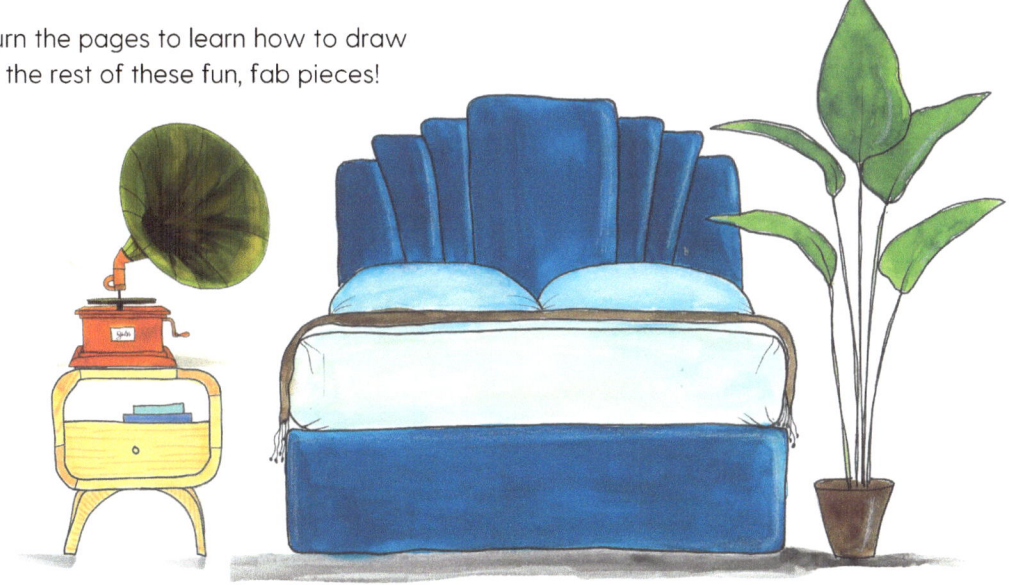

Step 4. Color or paint as desired! I used fountain pen ink!

ART DECO DESK

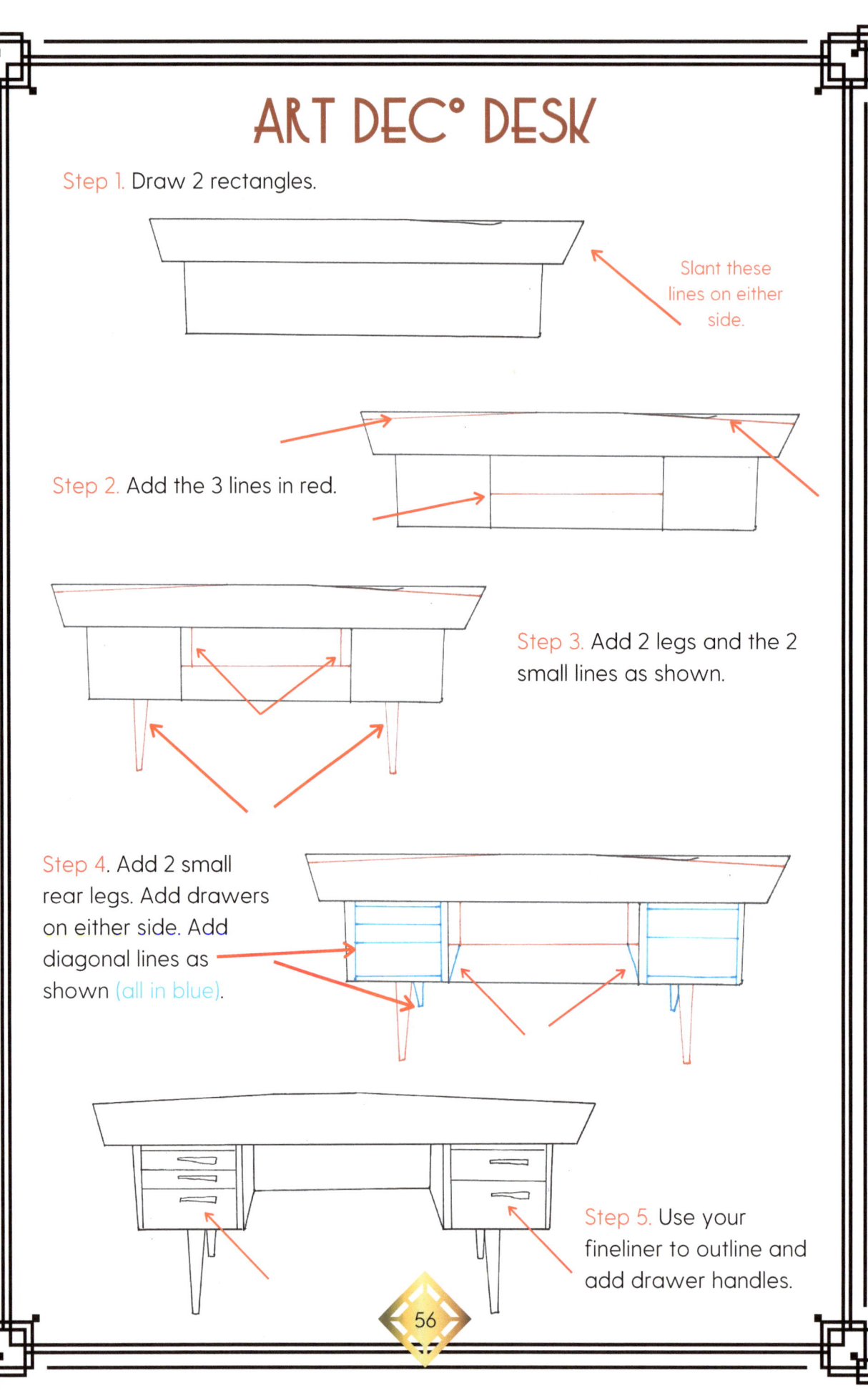

Step 1. Draw 2 rectangles.

Slant these lines on either side.

Step 2. Add the 3 lines in red.

Step 3. Add 2 legs and the 2 small lines as shown.

Step 4. Add 2 small rear legs. Add drawers on either side. Add diagonal lines as shown (all in blue).

Step 5. Use your fineliner to outline and add drawer handles.

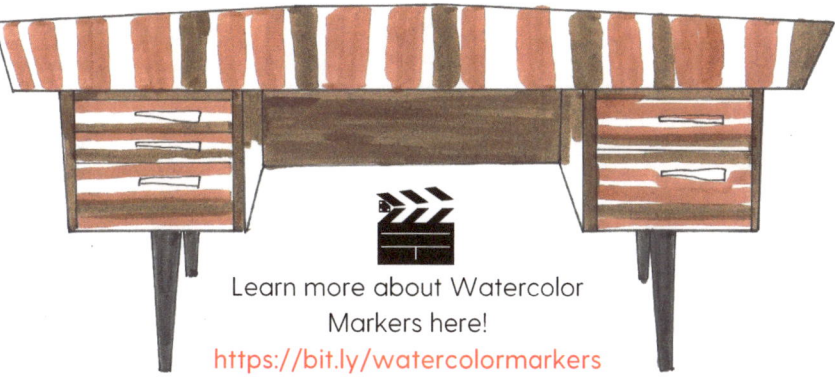

Learn more about Watercolor Markers here!
https://bit.ly/watercolormarkers

Step 6. In this project, I decided to use Watercolor Markers. If you'd like to try wet medium, I highly suggest you go for it! Starting with Watercolor paper is a must. Then draw the outline. Next, I'm using 2 shades of marker, like this. Use black watercolor marker for the legs.

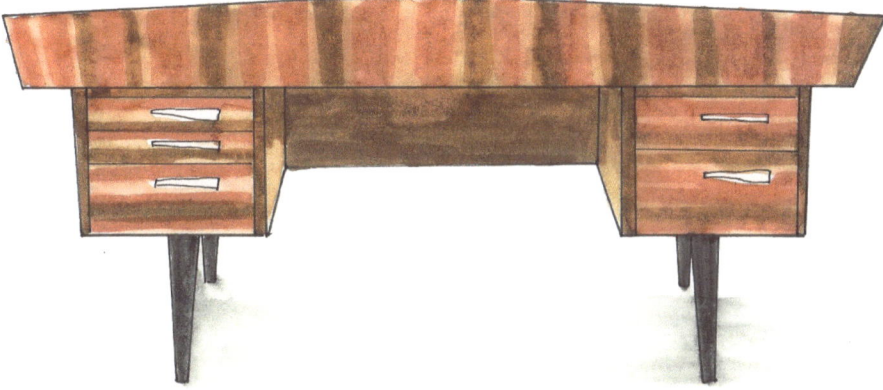

Step 7. Next, run a wet (with just plain water) brush over all the marker strokes. Let dry. Do a second coat of both markers and water brush. Let dry.

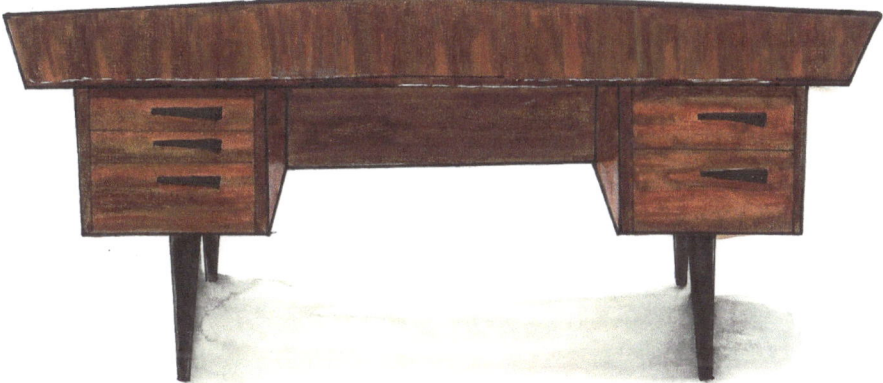

Step 8. Use colored pencils in similar shades to color in any spots that are too light. This accentuates the very real wood-grain look! Drag a wet brush through the black legs to create the shadow underneath. White gel pen for accents!

ART DECO DRESSER

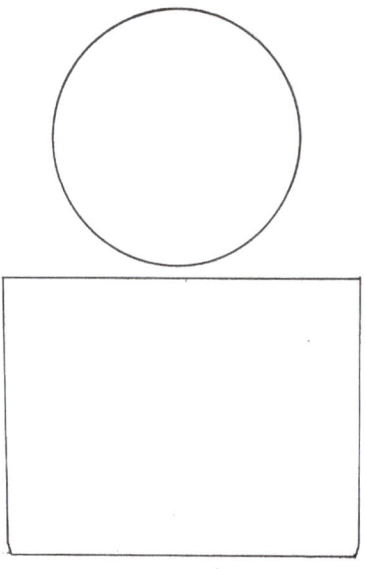

Step 1. Draw 1 large circle and rectangle underneath. Use a stencil to help.

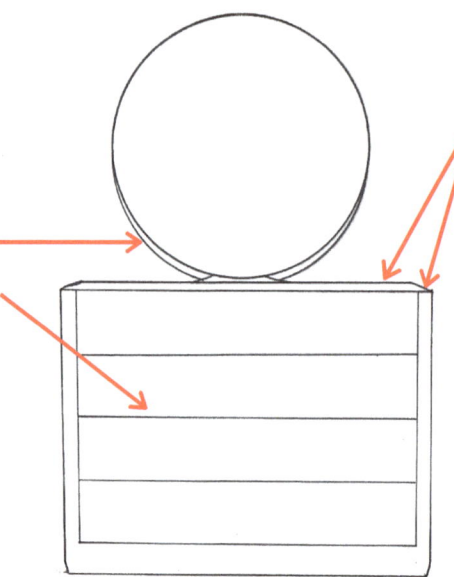

Step 2. Add the drawer lines, dresser depth and thin mirror frame.

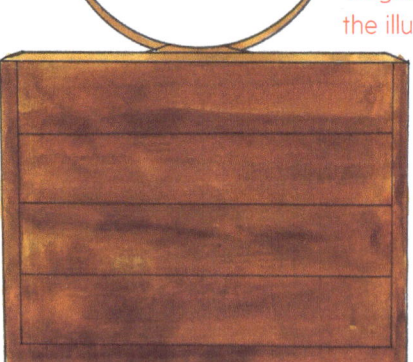

Step 3. Color in as desired! I am using fountain pen ink on hot press watercolor paper. Just one layer in a Pecan color is all I needed to do! Add short lines in circle.

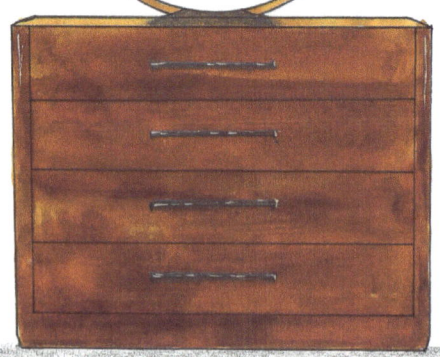

Drawing short, diagonal lines creates the illusion of a mirror.

Step 4. I drew the drawer handles using a soft pencil and then added a highlight using a white gel pen.

ART DECO COFFEE TABLE

Step 1. Draw a thin rectangle with a smaller block shape underneath.

Step 2 Add a single line up top. Add a second line at bottom.

Step 3. Add the few lines you see here in red.

Step 4. Finalize the end design with your favorite fineliner.

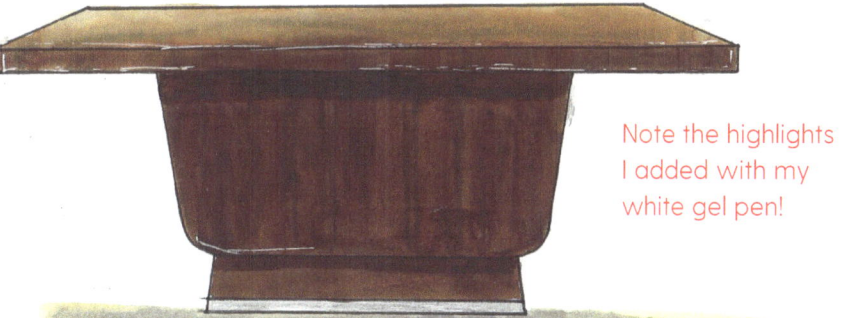

Note the highlights I added with my white gel pen!

Step 5. Color with your favorite art supply! I'm using fountain pen ink and colored pencil for this piece! Starting to think maybe Copics would have been even better! Whatever you choose, have fun with it!

MODERN DINING TABLE

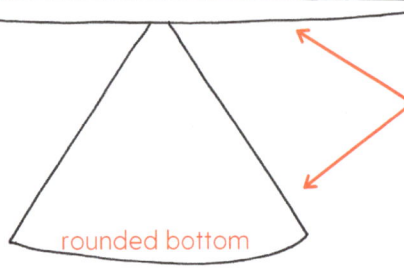

Step 1. Draw a super thin oval with a triangle underneath. Round the bottom of the triangle slightly.

To color this, as I am, you'll need 3 shades of grey.

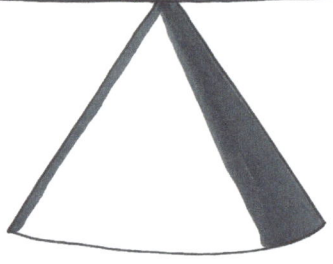

Step 2. Start with the darkest shade and color in places shown.

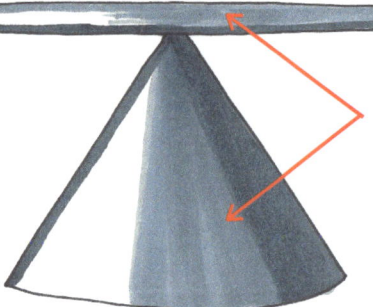

Step 3. Add the middle shade to the areas shown.

Step 4. Finish coloring the remaining spaces with the lightest color.

Add a floor if you wish!

MODERN DINING CHAIRS

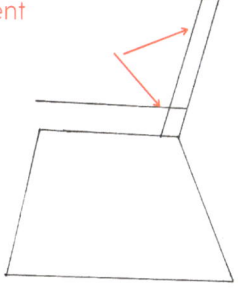
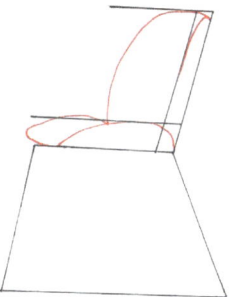
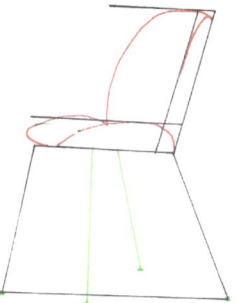

Step 1. Draw 3 horizontal lines. Connect ends as shown.

Step 2. Draw 2 lines as shown, make them parallel to the original lines.

Step 3. Draw 4 curved lines (shown in red).

Step 4. Draw 2 more chair legs (green).

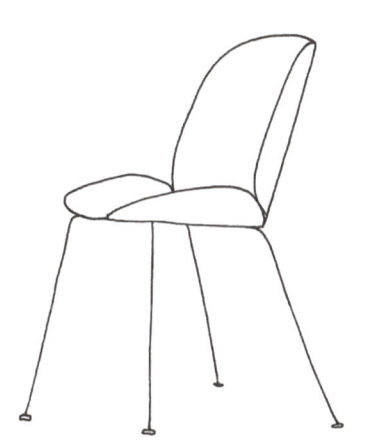
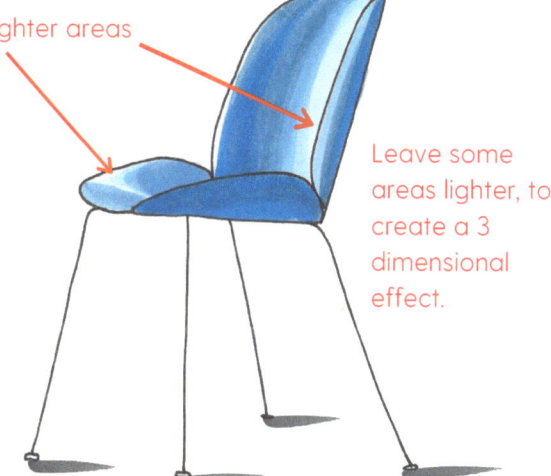

Step 5. Outline the final shape.

Step 6. Color! Add feet shadows if desired.

Leave some areas lighter, to create a 3 dimensional effect.

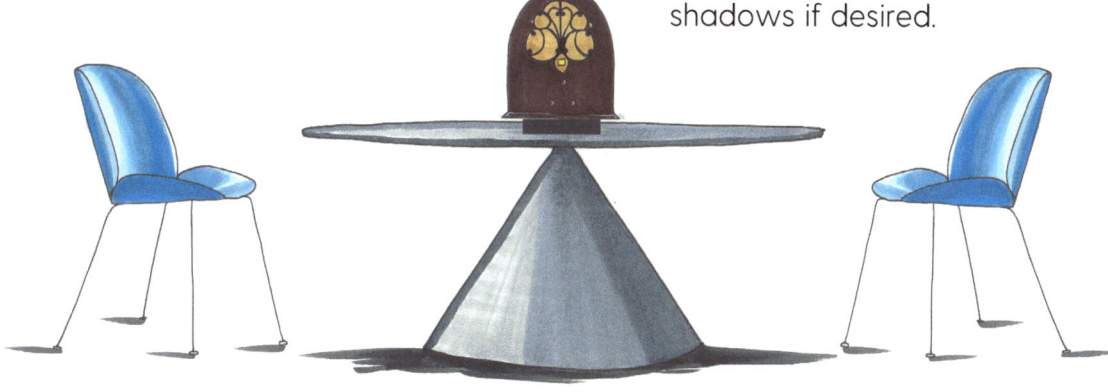

Try drawing a little scene! So fun!

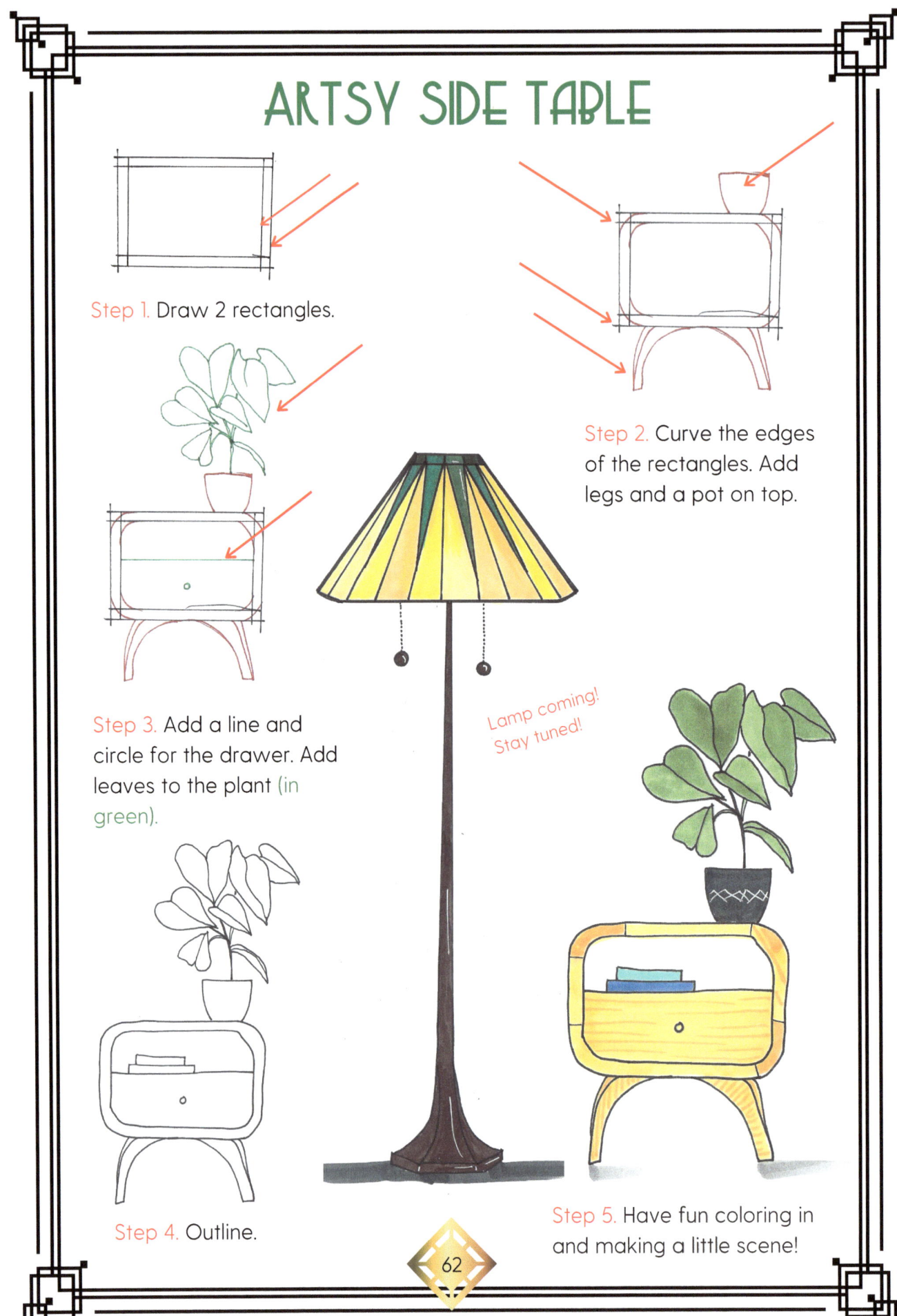

ICONIC MIRROR

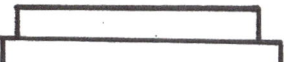

Step 1. Draw 2 narrow rectangles, stacked.

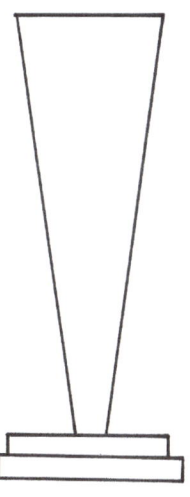

Step 2. On the 2 rectangles, add a large, inverted triangular shape.

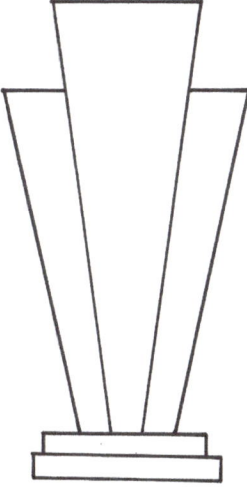

Step 3. Add 2 more rectangular shapes on either side.

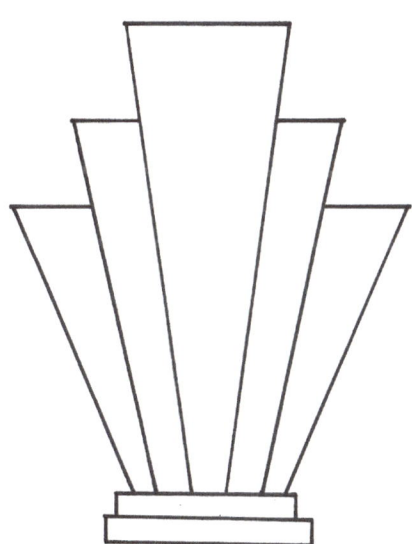

Step 4. Flank yet one more pair of rectangular lines on either side.
Use a ruler to help keep your lines exact, and straight.

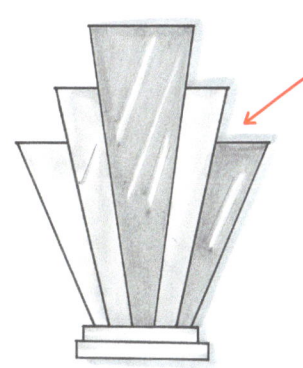

Step 5. Color in grey. Leave streaks of white to infer reflection.

Two fun color options to make mirrors look more realistic.

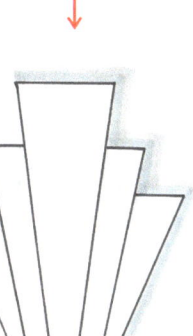

Or, leave white and just draw lines in grey.

ICONIC SCONCE

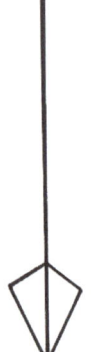 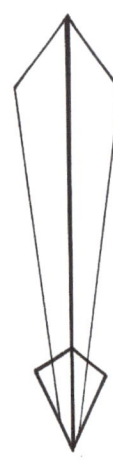 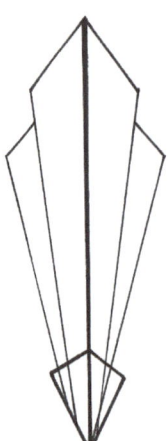 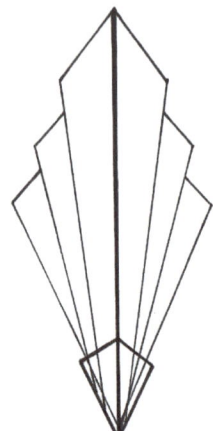

Step 1. Draw an arrow shape. Use a ruler to help!

Step 2. Add lines on either side. Diagonals at the top.

Step 3. Add 2 more lines on either side.

Step 4. Add 2 more lines on either side yet again.

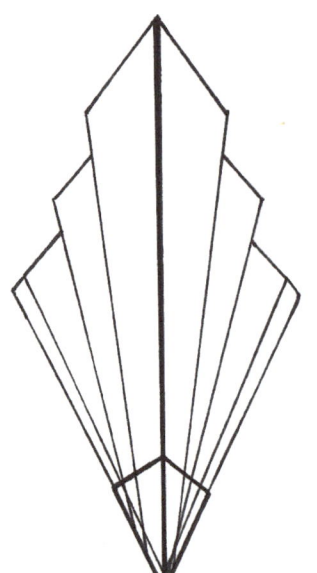 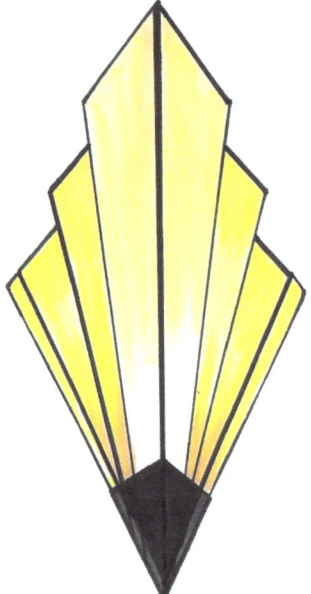 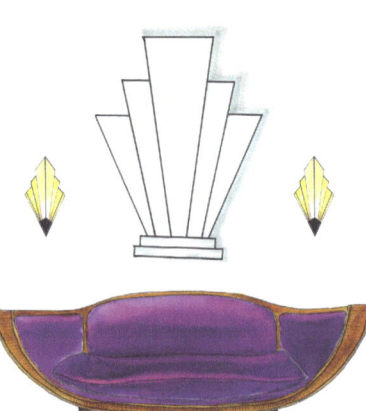

Step 5. Add the last set of lines out from the bottom to last set of diagonals.

Step 6. Color!

Step 7. Dream!

TIFFANY LAMP

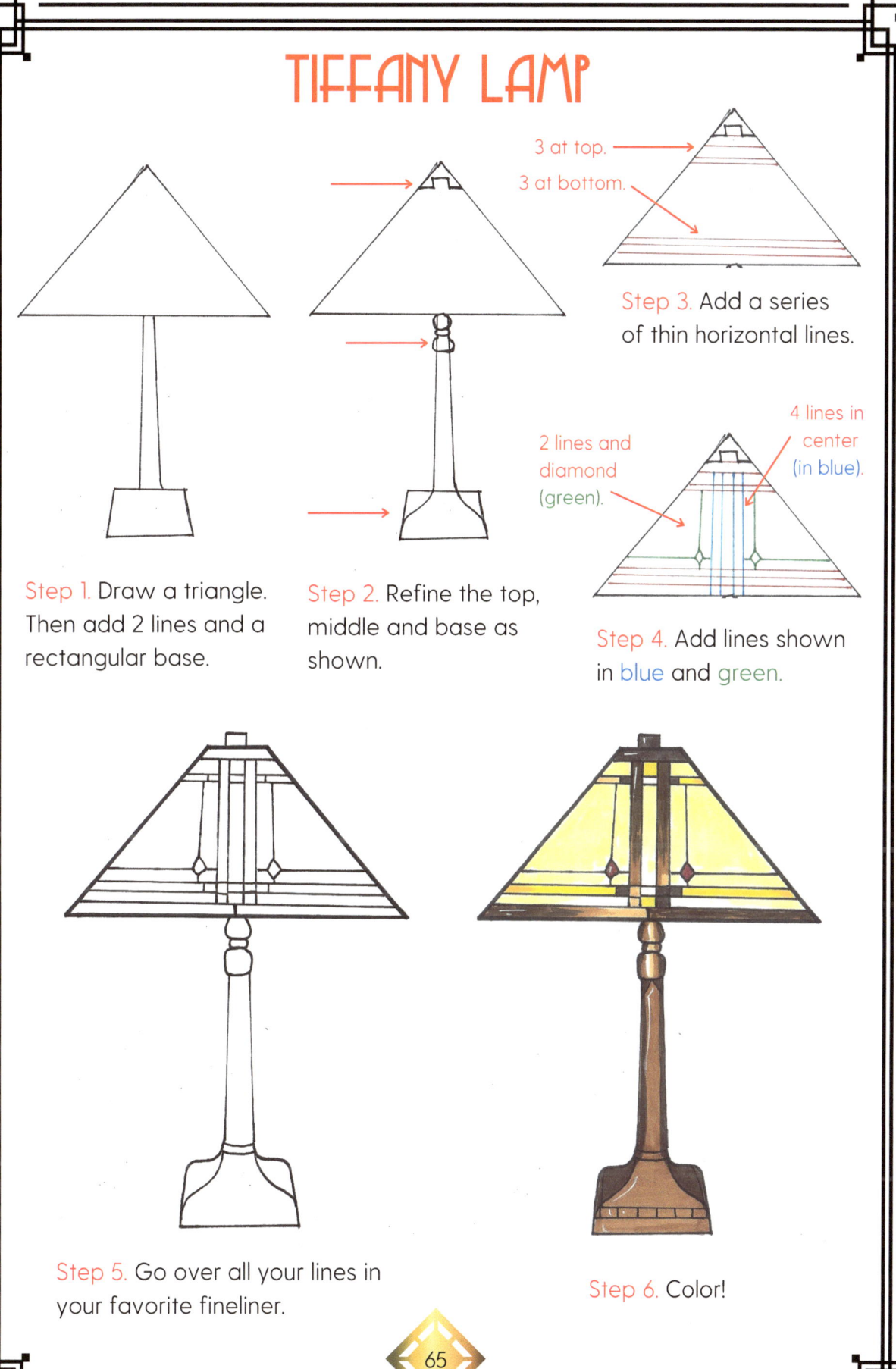

Step 1. Draw a triangle. Then add 2 lines and a rectangular base.

Step 2. Refine the top, middle and base as shown.

Step 3. Add a series of thin horizontal lines.

Step 4. Add lines shown in blue and green.

Step 5. Go over all your lines in your favorite fineliner.

Step 6. Color!

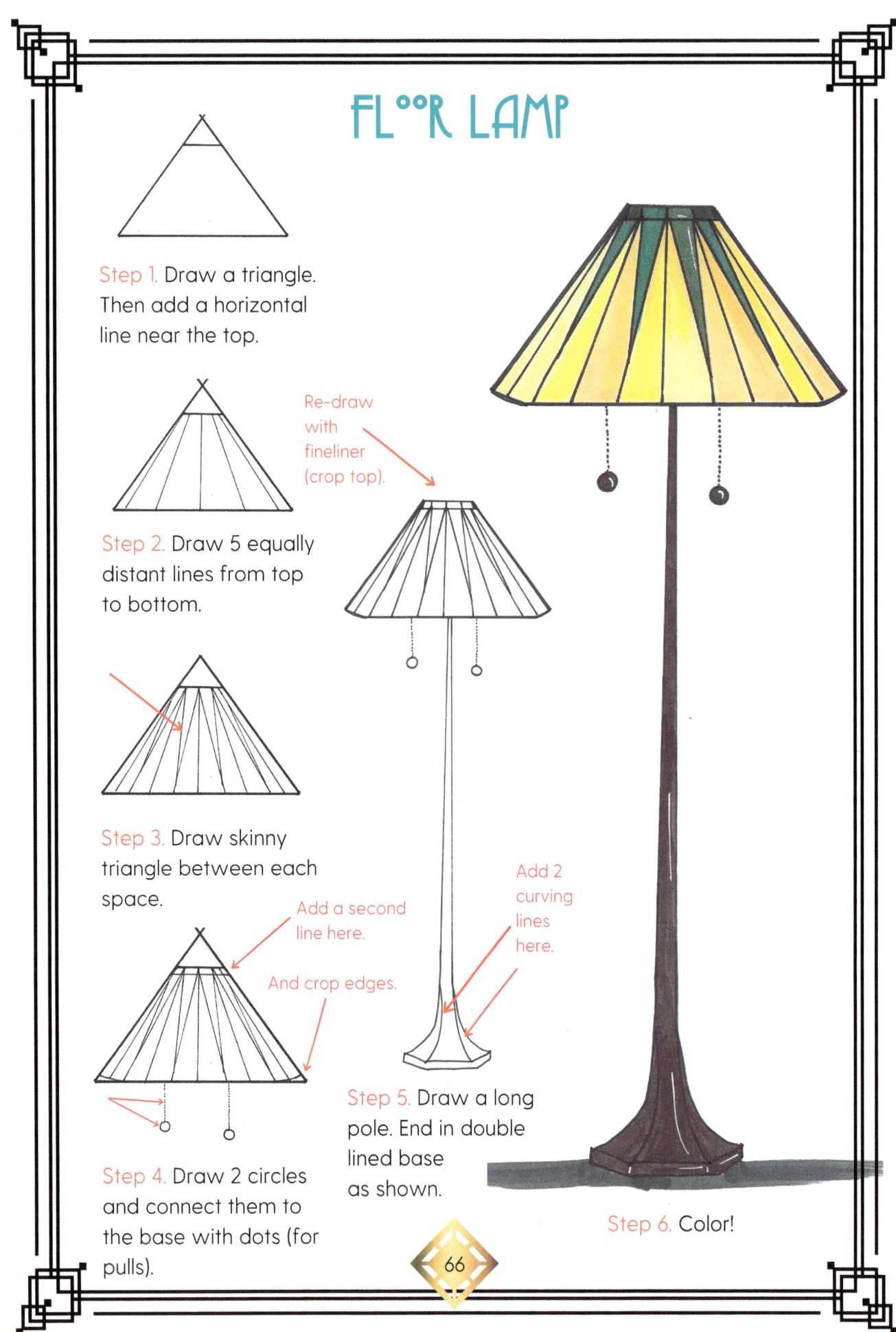

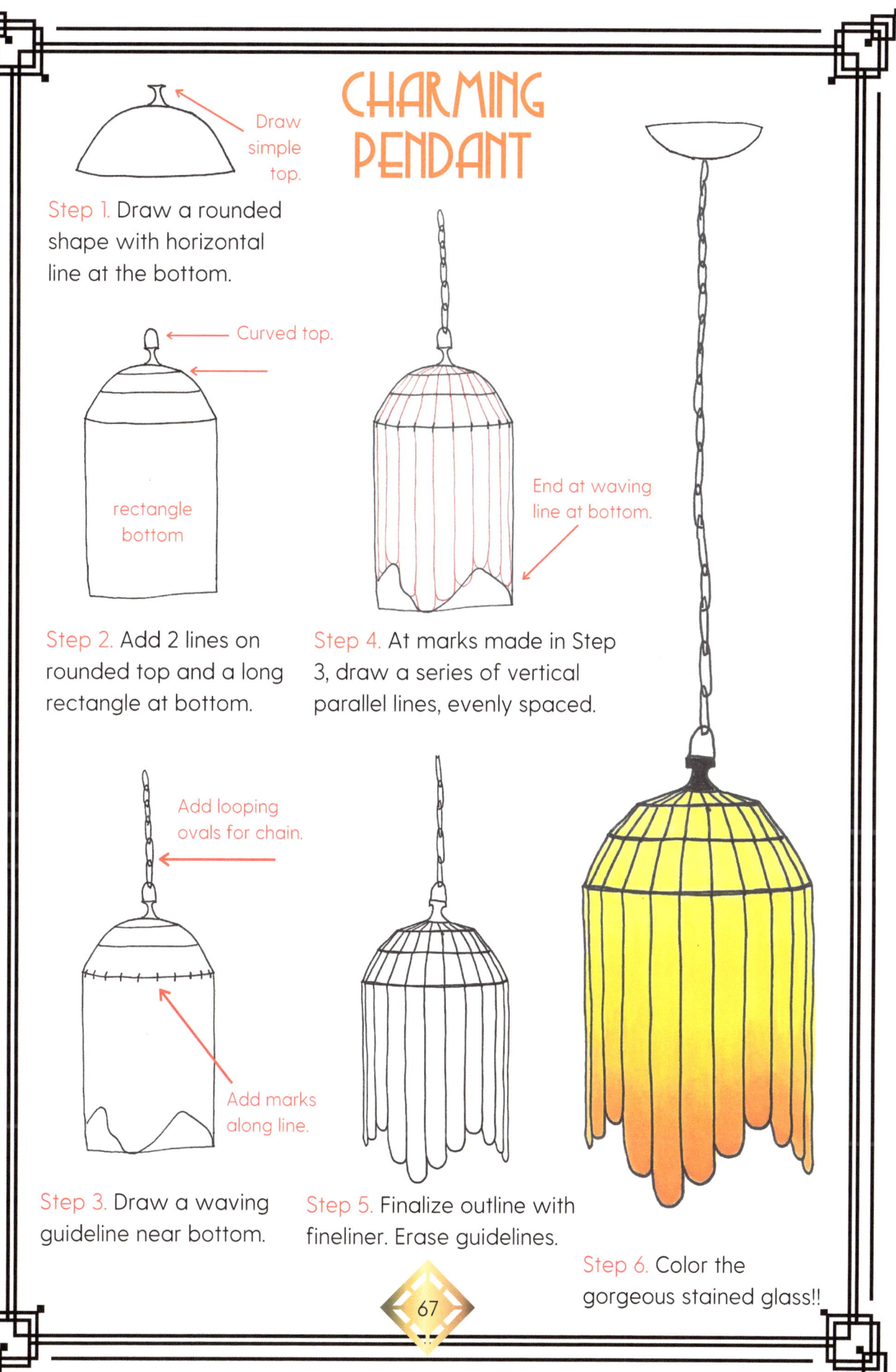

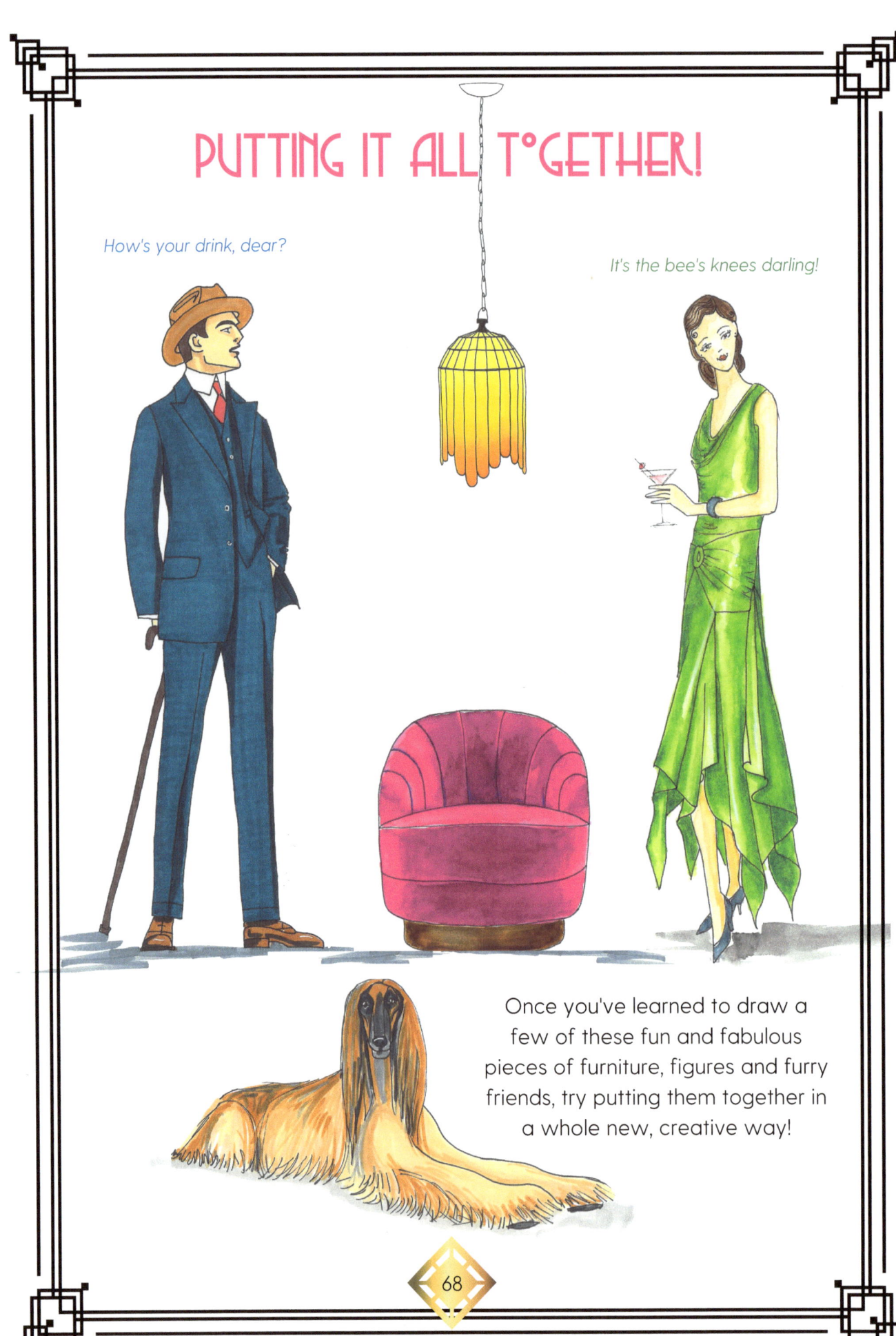

TECHNOLOGY

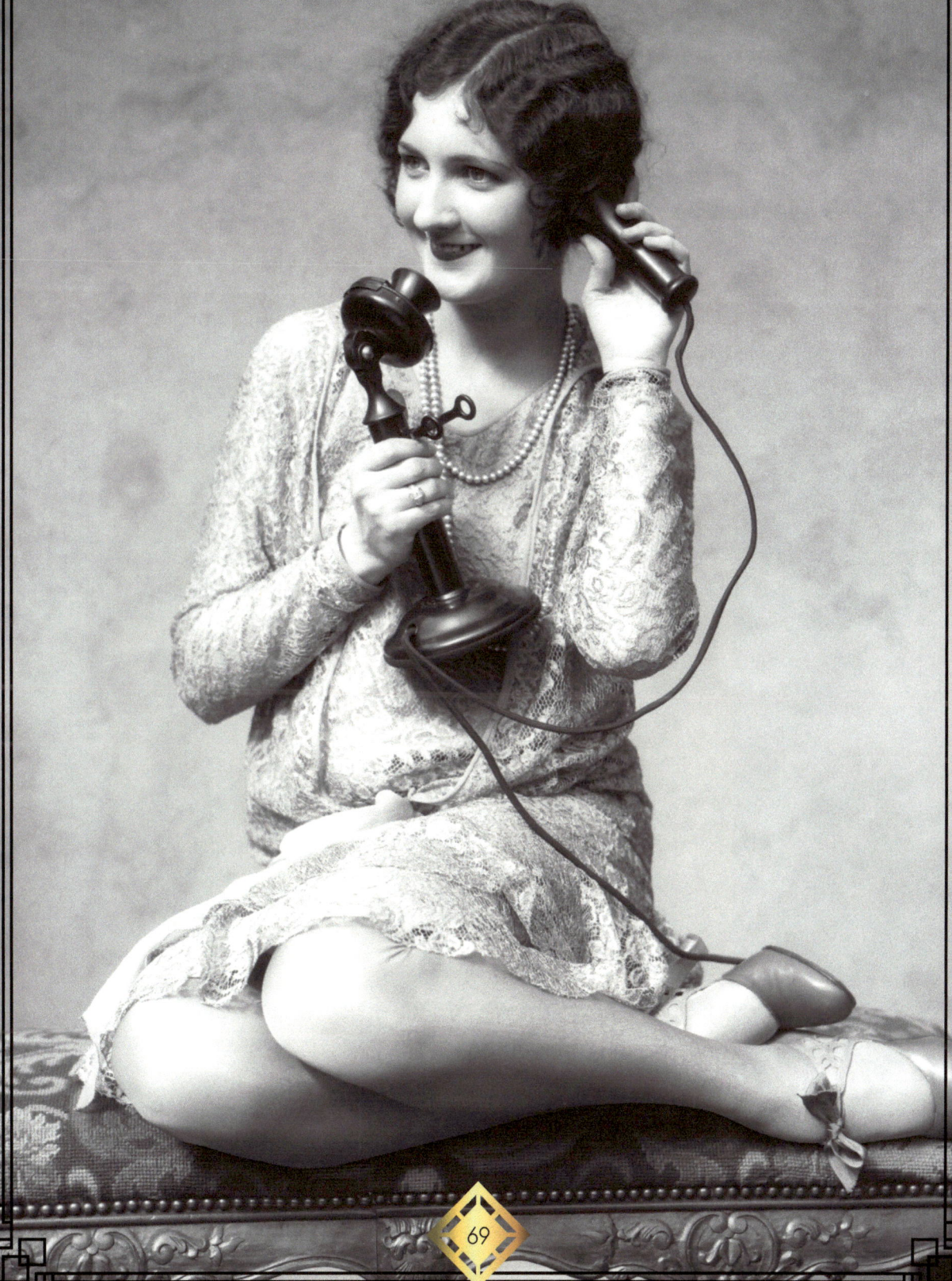

Among the many exciting developments of the Art Deco era was the first radio program which was launched in 1920. Radios were also commercially available for the first time (although they cost a pretty penny at $400-$800 each!).

1922 introduced the first silent pictures and in 1926 the first moving pictures - in color! Thanks to advances in technology, entertainment in many forms became widely available to the masses.

Gorgeous and iconic candlestick telephones were also widely in use until the mid 1930's until replaced by the more "modern" cradle based phones that were used until the 21st century.

And yes, we will be drawing both!

Other forms of popular technology during this time were the gramophone and phonograph. Both of these were used during the Art Deco period.

The last gramophone was manufactured in 1929 and was eventually replaced by the turntable (or phonograph) both of which would remain popular throughout the 1930's and 40's.

RADIO

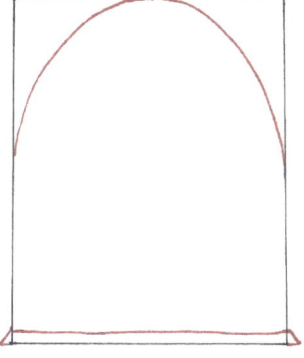 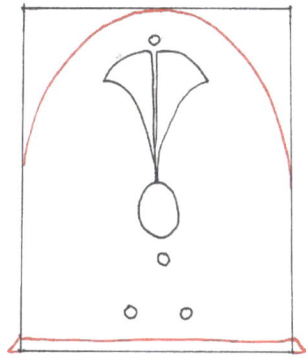 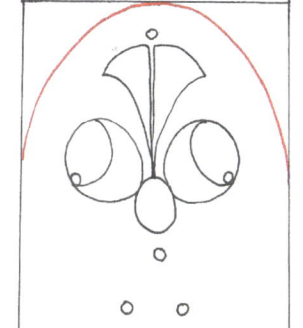

Step 1. Draw a rectangle. Add curved lines within. Then add a strip along the bottom for base.

Step 2. Add 5 circles. Draw decorative curvy triangles in center.

Step 3. Add more circles on either side. Try to be symmetrical if you can.

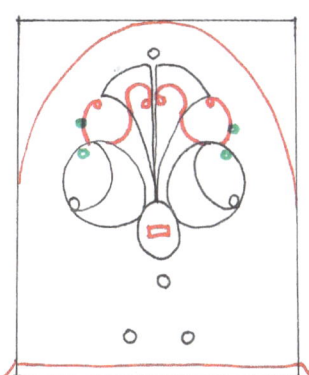 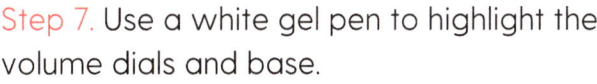

Step 6. Color the entire radio. Use a lighter color for the speaker part. (In my drawing, it is beige).

Step 5. Finalize your sketch. Erase guidelines. Make the decorative swirly parts bold and black!

Step 4. Add some swirlies (in red) and some dots (green).

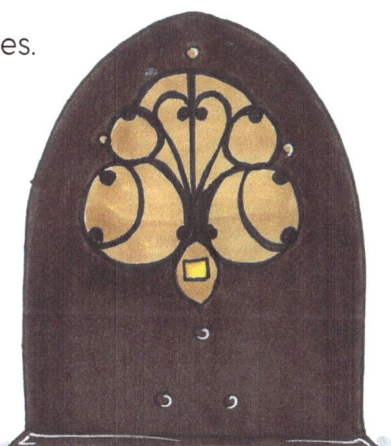

Step 7. Use a white gel pen to highlight the volume dials and base.

CANDELSTICK TELEPHONE

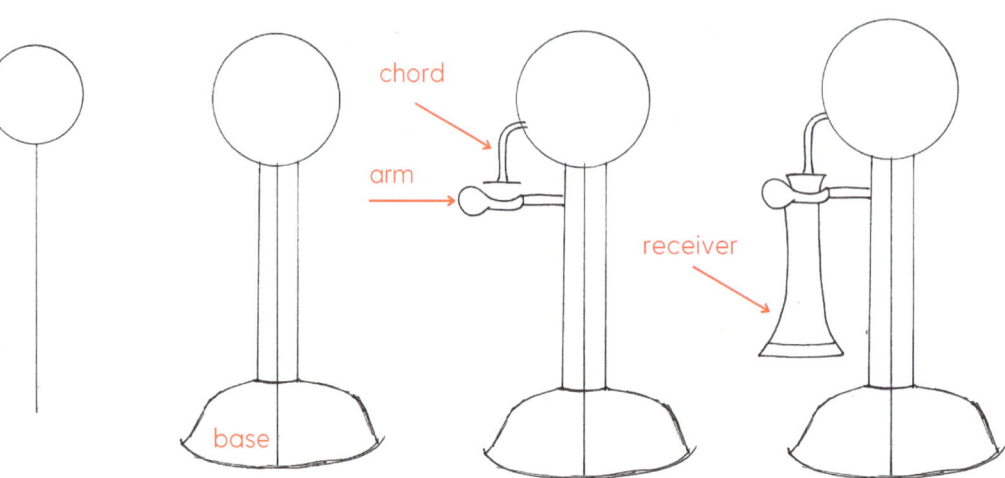

Step 1. Draw a circle and straight line from center.

Step 2. Draw the base and 2 lines parallel to first.

Step 3. Draw the arm and chord as shown.

Step 4. Draw bell shape (receiver) off of arm piece.

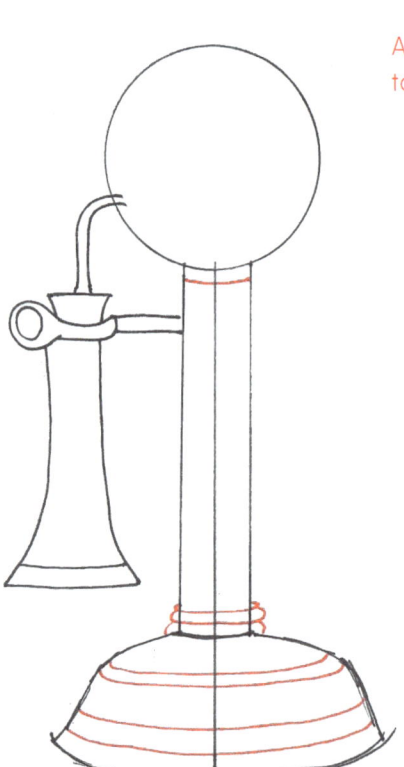

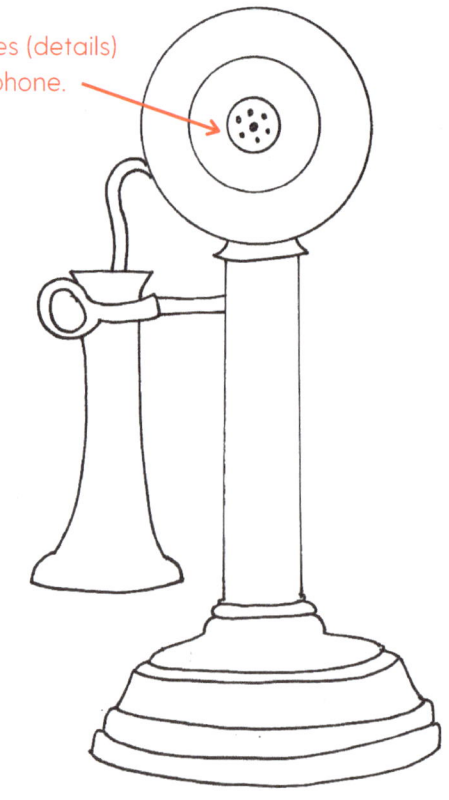

Step 5. Draw accent lines as shown in red.

Step 6. Do final outline in fineliner. Erase guidelines. Add details to microphone

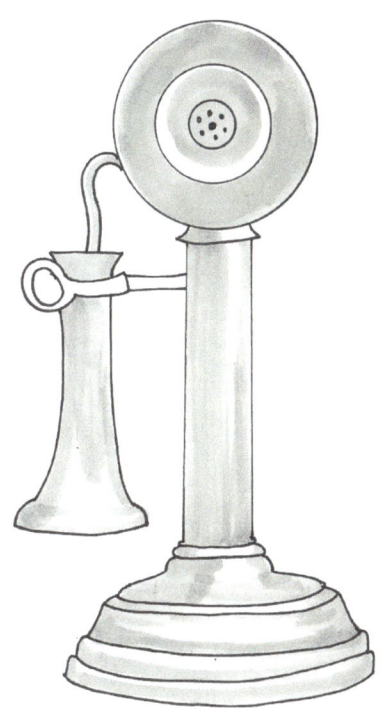

Step 7. Apply a base coat of light grey. Leave highlighted areas white.

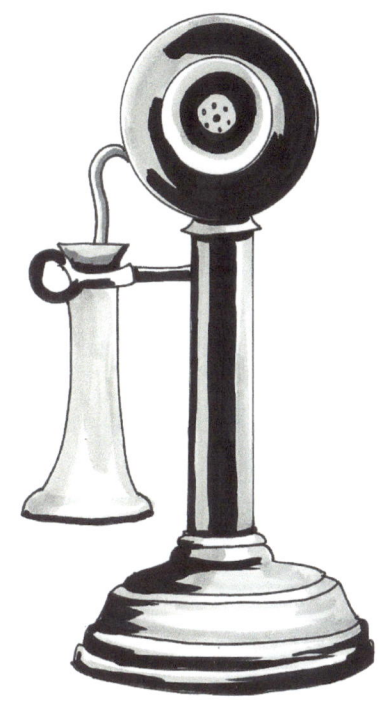

Step 8. Apply black to areas shown.

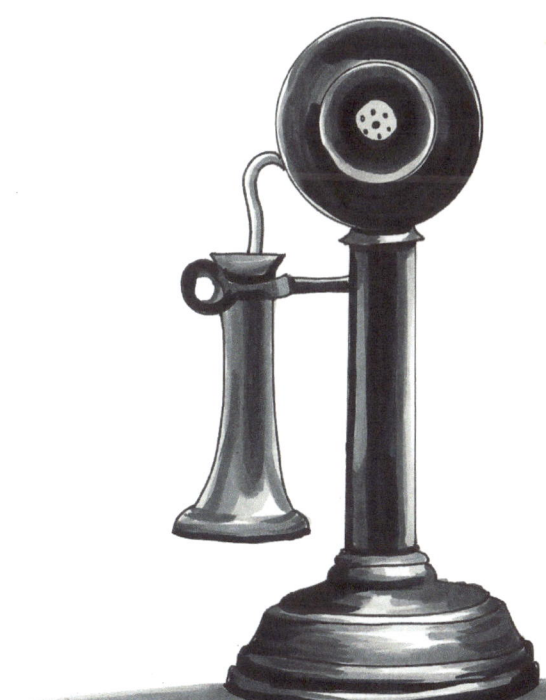

Step 9. Use a dark grey to blend between light grey and black areas.

Step 10. Allow your imagination to dream up new drawing ideas!

OLD TIMEY PHONE

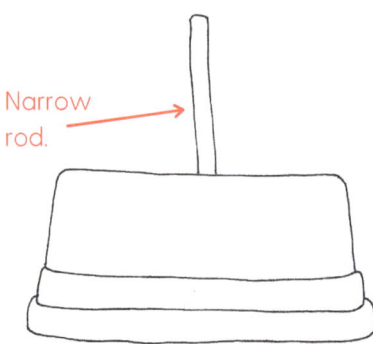

Narrow rod.

Step 1. Draw a 3 stepped rectangle with a narrow rod coming up from the middle.

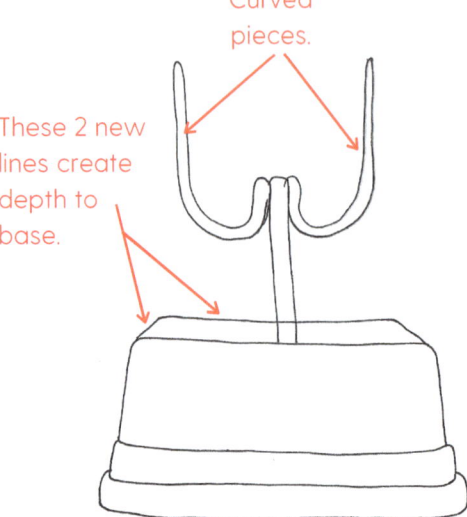

Curved pieces.

These 2 new lines create depth to base.

Step 2. Add 2 lines off the base. Draw 2 curved pieces on either side of the middle rod part.

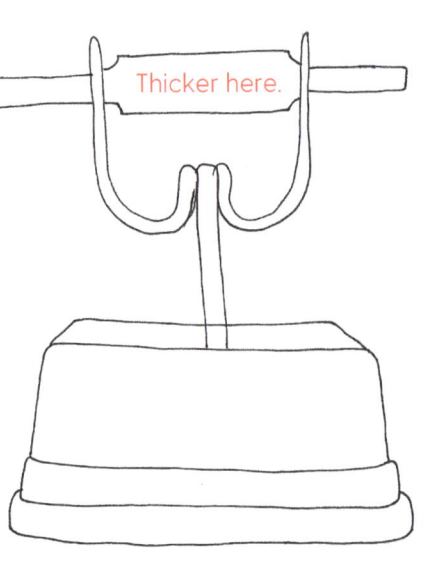

Thicker here.

Step 3. Draw a piece across the top where the center part is thicker than the ends. Ends should extend just beyond the widest part of the base (see red dashed line).

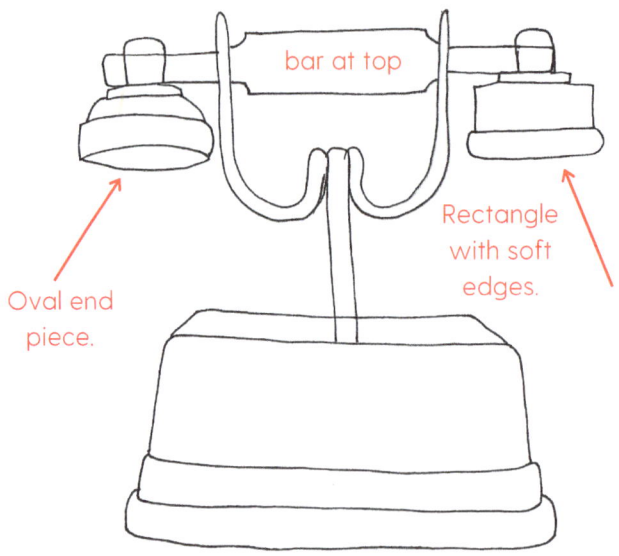

bar at top

Oval end piece.

Rectangle with soft edges.

Step 4. Draw a series of rectangles on either side of bar at top. The left side should end in an oval, the right side ends in a rounded edged rectangle.

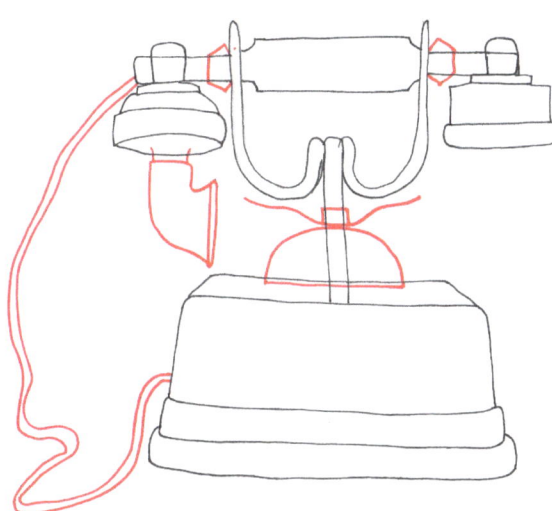 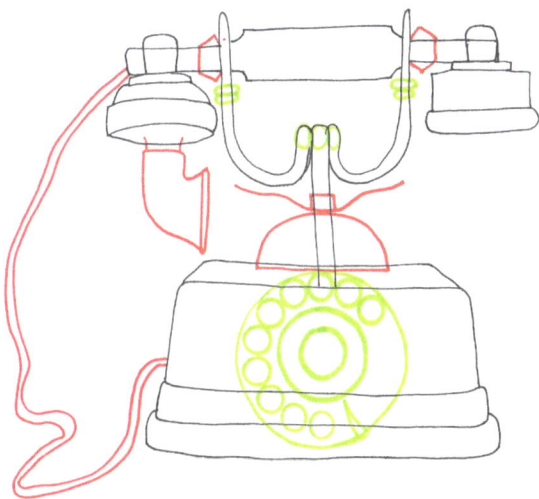

Step 5. Draw the mouthpiece, bell, chord and decorative pieces (all shown here in red).

Step 6. Add just a few decorative pieces (shown in green). Then, using a circle template, draw a series of circles to create the dial mechanism.

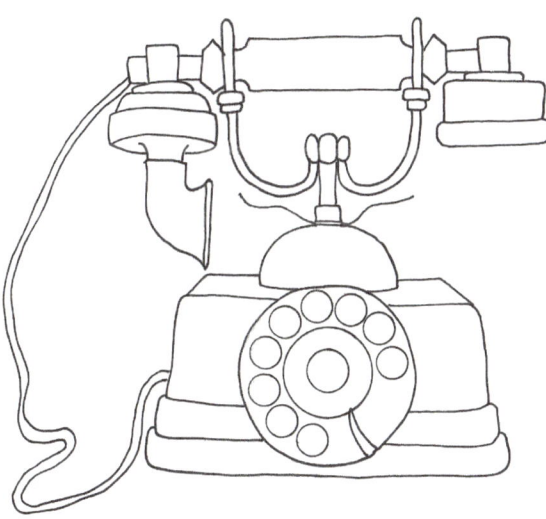 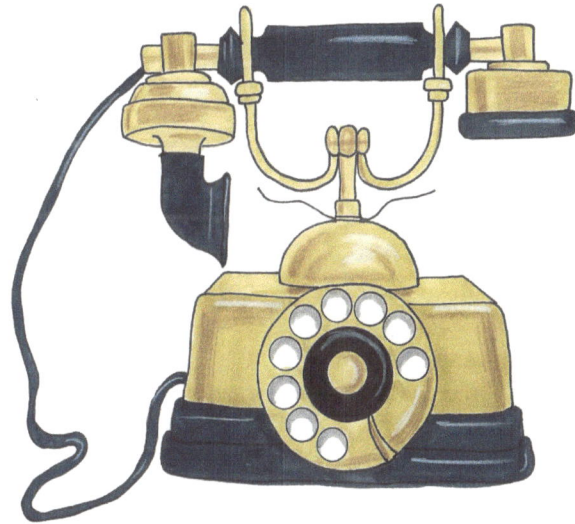

Step 7. Outline your final drawing with your favorite fineliner. Erase all your guidelines and extraneous lines.

Step 8. Color or paint with your favorite art supplies! Be sure to add highlights of white to make your drawing look 3 dimensional!

THE GRAMOPHONE

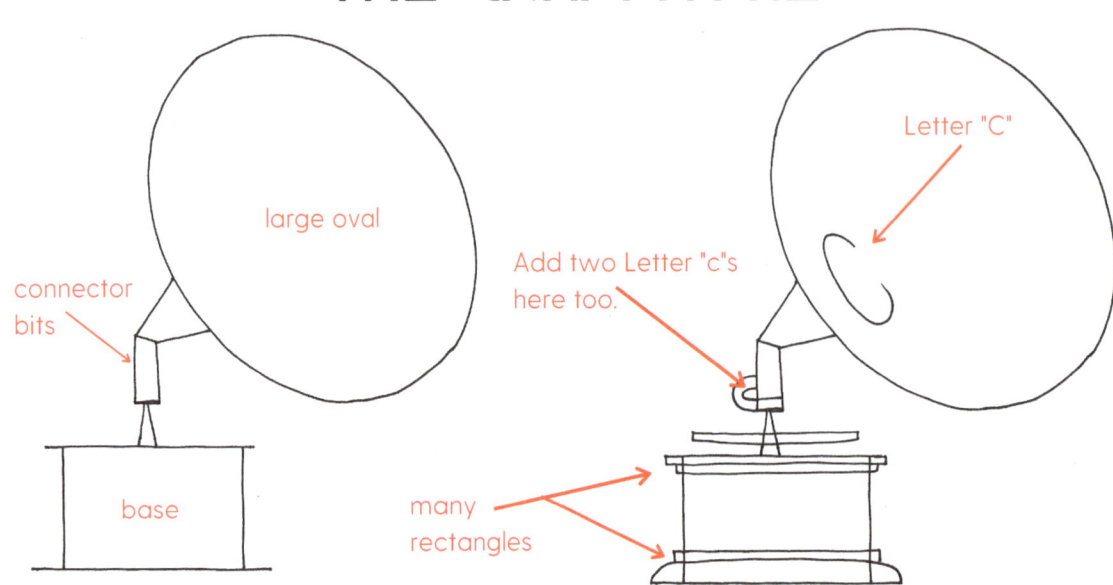

Step 1. Start with a large oval. Draw basic shape connector bits. Add a rectangle base.

Step 2. Draw a letter "C" off center of the oval. Add a series of thin rectangles at top and bottom of base.

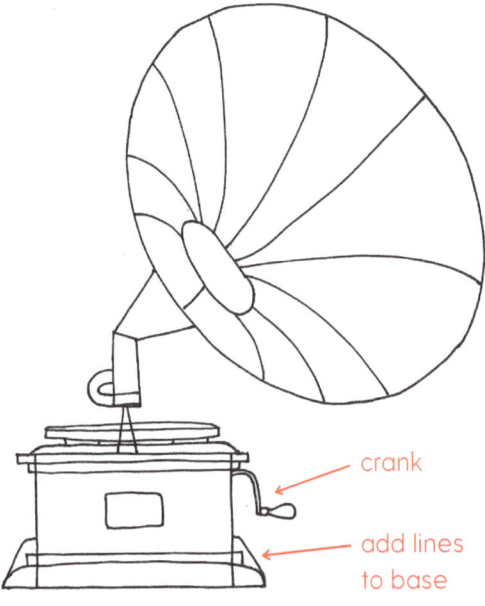

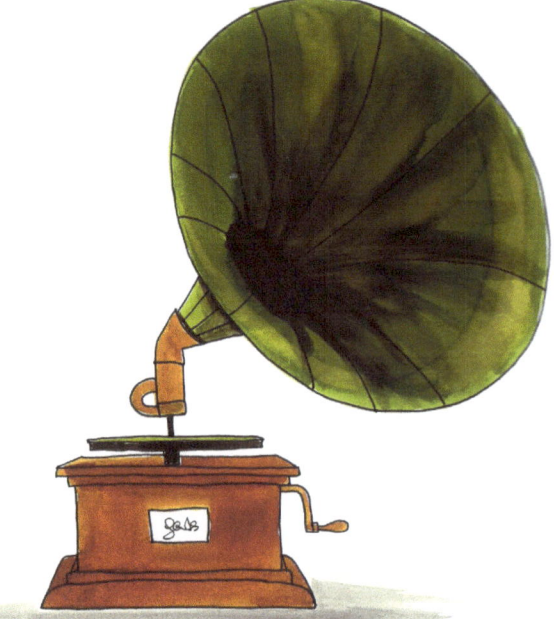

Step 3. Add the crank on the right and a rectangle on the front. Draw curved lines coming out from center.

Step 4. Color or paint your vintage gramophone! I used ink for this one!

Gramophones came in all kinds of designs, colors and materials so feel free to get fancy!

76

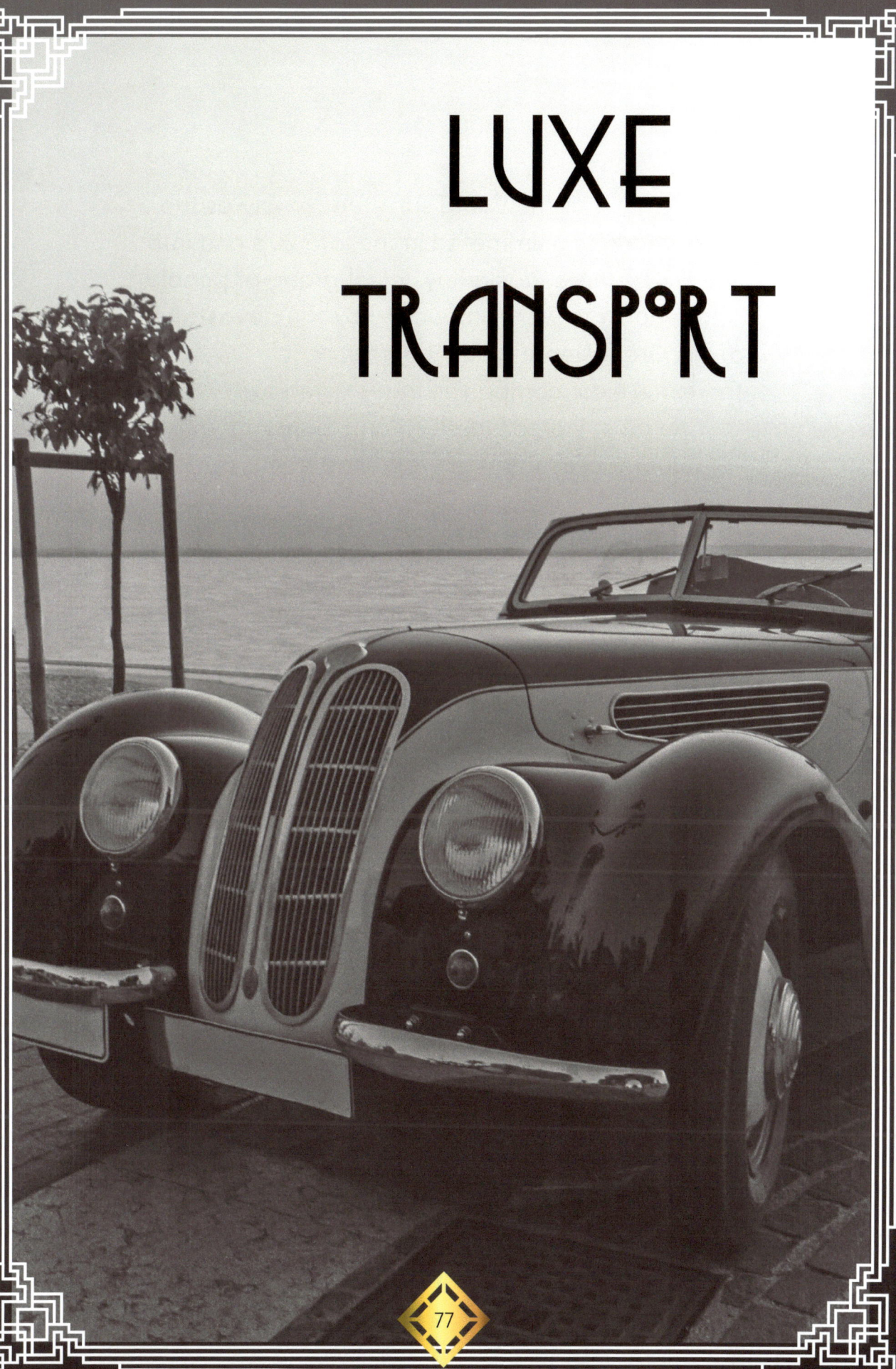

While most of the world suffered terribly as the stock markets plummeted in the late 20's and into the 1930's, there was a tiny select group of people whose pockets were untouched by the devastation of the Great Depression. And, fortunately for them, there were car companies that existed to serve up the most incredible, sleek and extravagant automobiles that the world had ever seen.

Cars of the Art Deco period were all about style. Swooping curves, bold colors, long hoods and dramatic accents were built and designed to make a statement and make a statement they did!

The Art Deco artistic movement, as you've seen already in the clothing, furnishings, and even canine friends, is about extravagance, bold, geometric shapes and flashy, jewel toned colors. So it should come as no surprise that the same characteristics should apply to the vehicles of the ultra-rich!

Drawing these sweeping fenders and elongated forms is pure fun.

Grab your favorite bold mediums and meet me at your art table! I'm not normally a car person, but these are just too good to pass up!

1929 BUGATTI

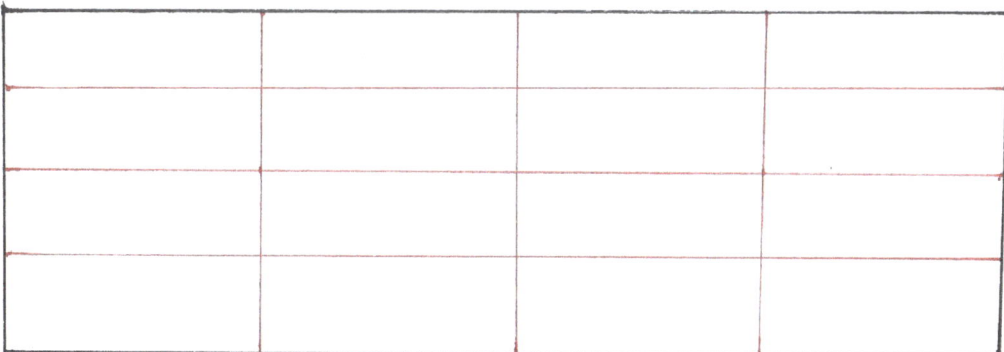

Step 1. Draw a rectangle approximately 20 x 7 cm. Divide that into equal **Quadrants** as shown. Then proceed to Step 2.

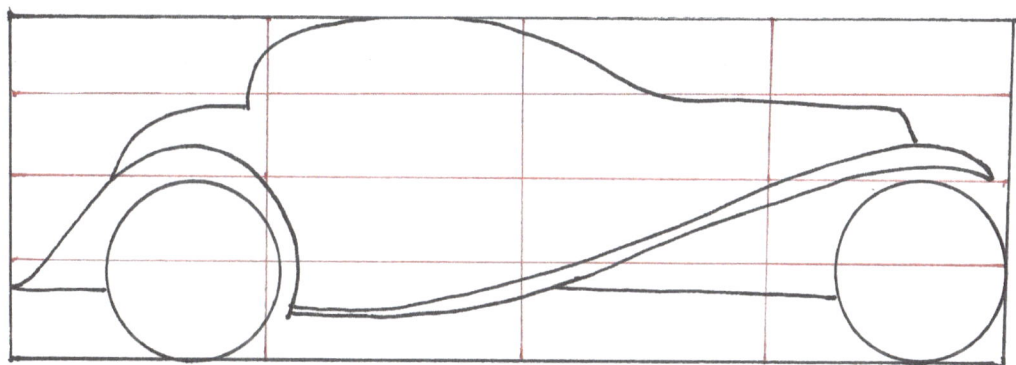

Step 2. Using the **Quadrant** lines, sketch the shape of the car as shown. Use the grid lines to help you determine the placement of each line and circle.

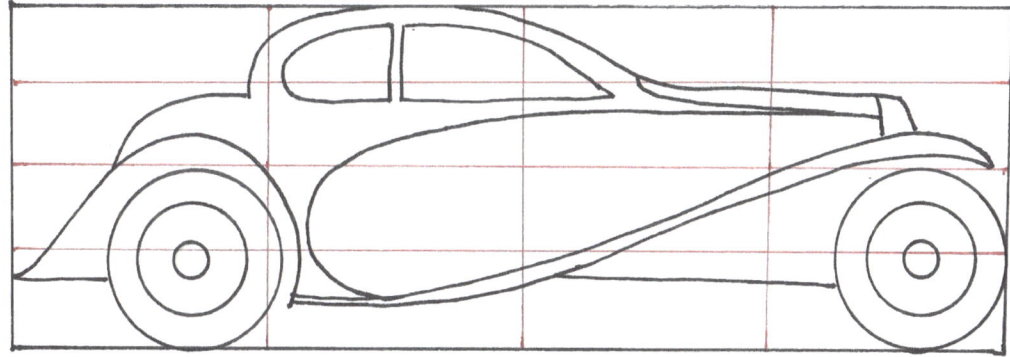

Step 3 Add interior tire circles, the windows, and the 2 side curved accents.

1929 BUGATTI

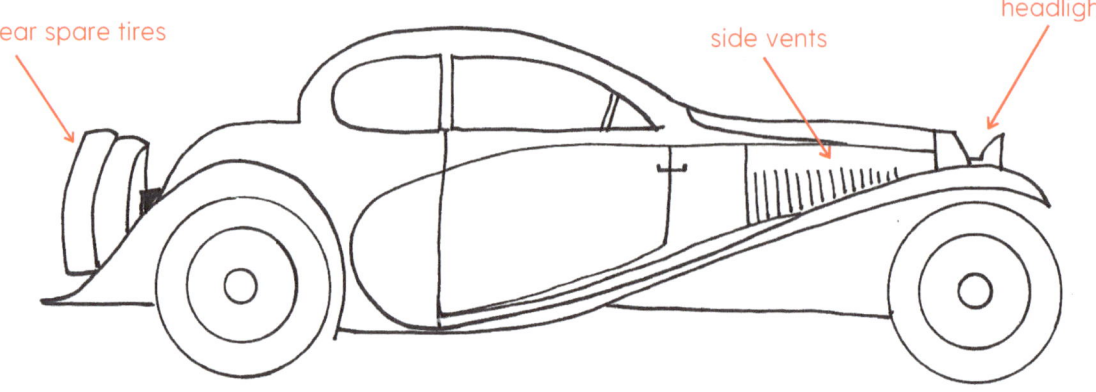

Step 4. Draw the final version with your favorite fineliner. Then add the little details like the vents along the side, the rear spare tires, and the front light.

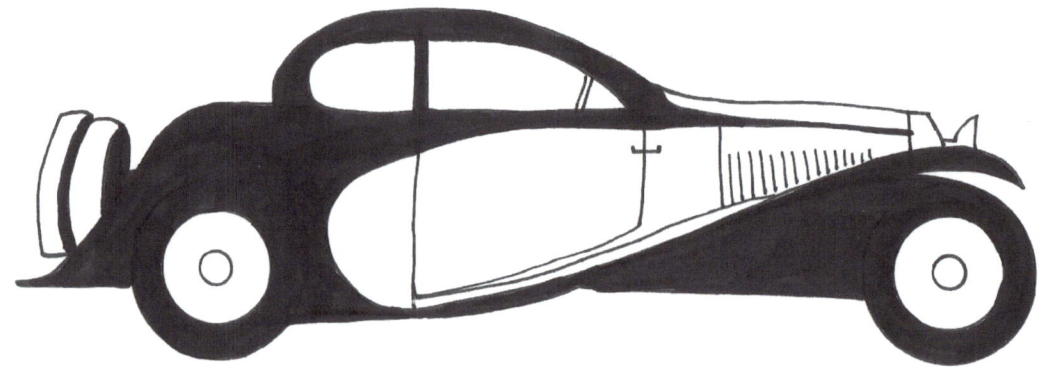

Step 5. Use black to color all the areas shown.

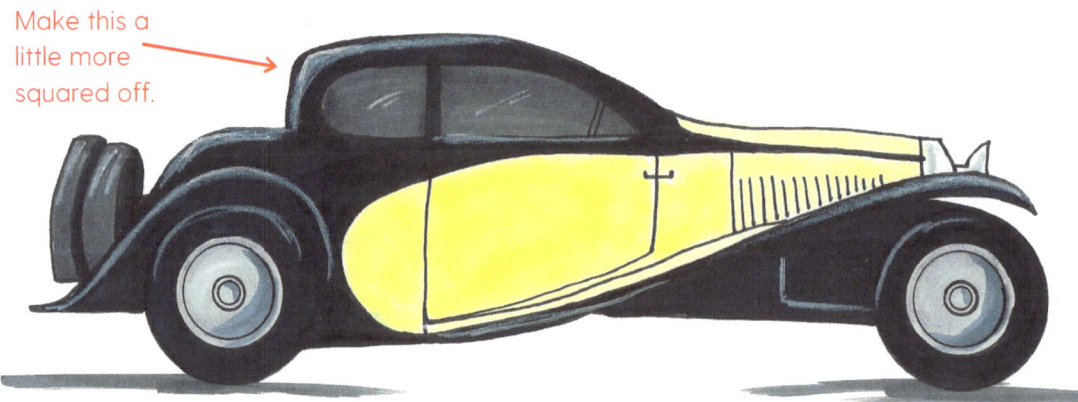

Step 6 Use light yellow to color in the side and top areas. Use grey for the windows and tires. Add white color pencil to create dimension!

1934 ESDEL FORD MODEL 40

Step 1. Draw a rectangle approximately 23 x 6 cm. Divide that into 6 equal spaces. Then proceed to Step 2.

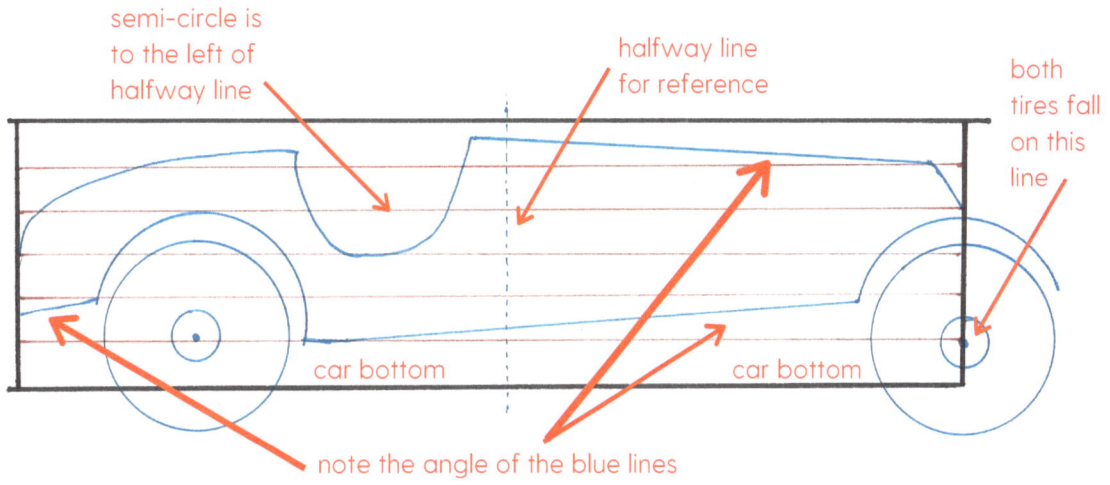

Step 2. Using the lines to help you, sketch the tires first (about 4.5 cm in diameter) of the car as shown. Use the red reference lines to help you draw the blue lines of the car in accurately. Pay careful attention to the angles of lines.

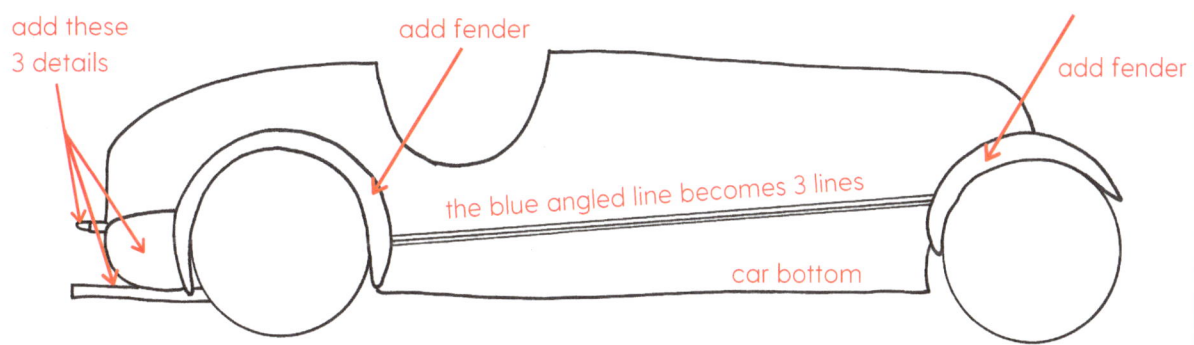

Step 3. Redraw the outline with your fineliner and add details shown. Note where the car bottom is in all the steps to help you locate the overall wheel and detail proportions.

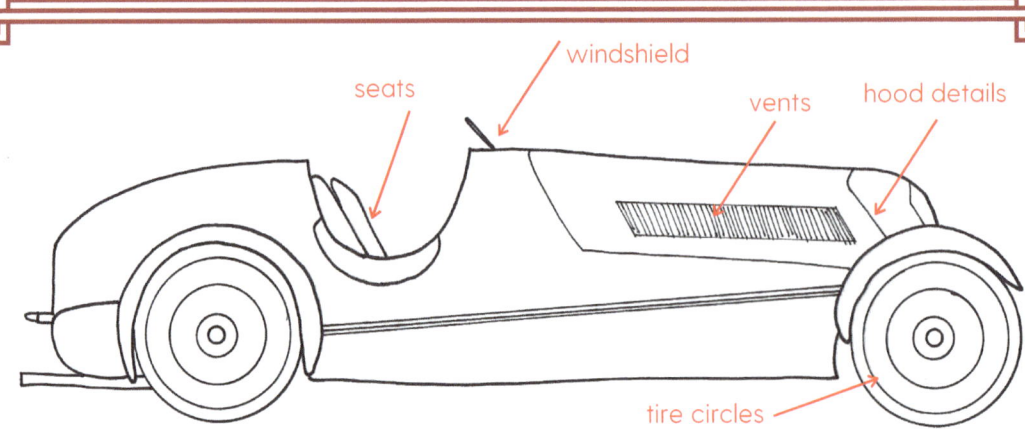

Step 4. Now add more details. The tires get more circles inside. There are 2 seats, a windshield, a hood and vents. Outline all your final details with a fineliner until the look is complete.

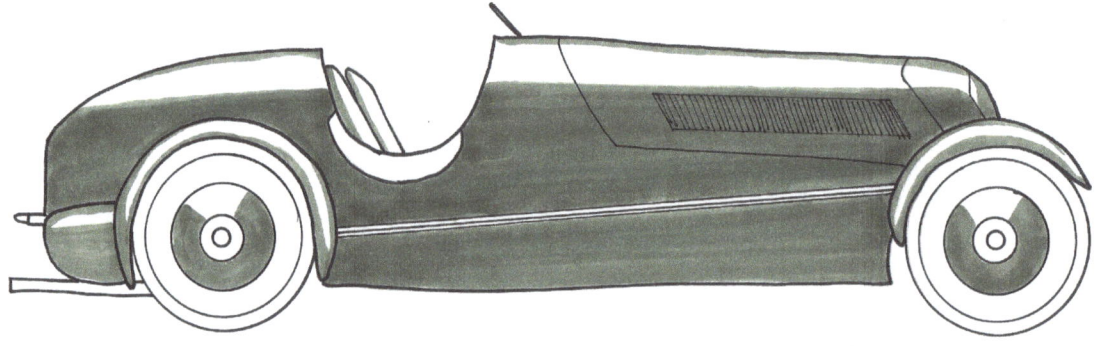

Step 5. Use a dark green marker to color in the areas shown. Take care to leave the other areas white to show reflection.

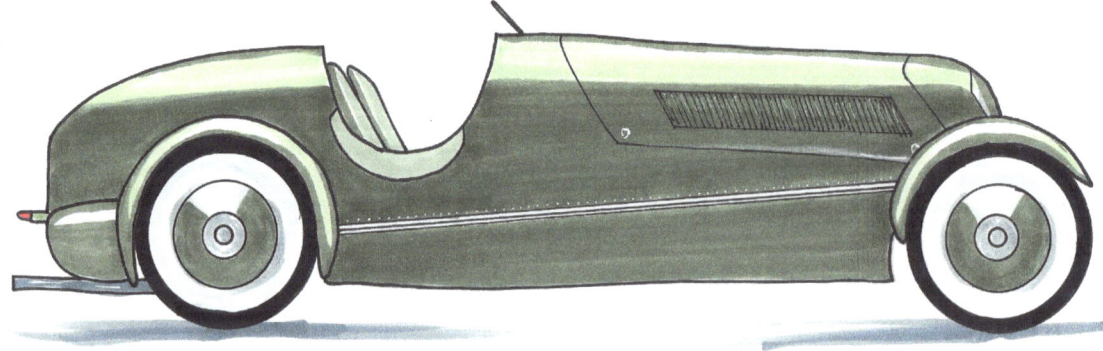

Step 6 Use a light green shade to color in reflected areas and black for the tires. Add a road in grey and get ready to go for one hell of a ride!!!

TALBOT-LAGO, 1938

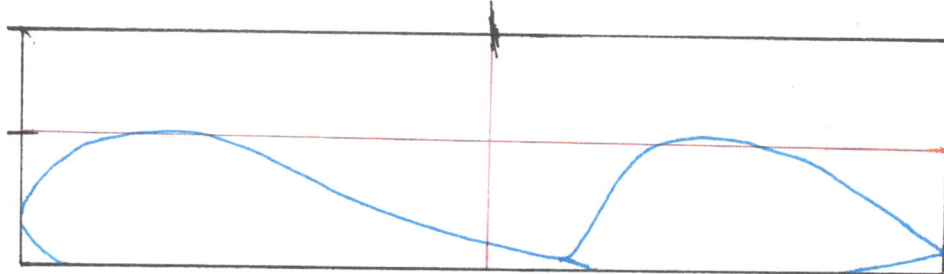

Step 1. Draw a long, thin rectangle. Divide that in half, both vertically and horizontally (red guidelines). Then draw the two swooping lines (shown in blue). Note where they begin and end within the **Quadrants**.

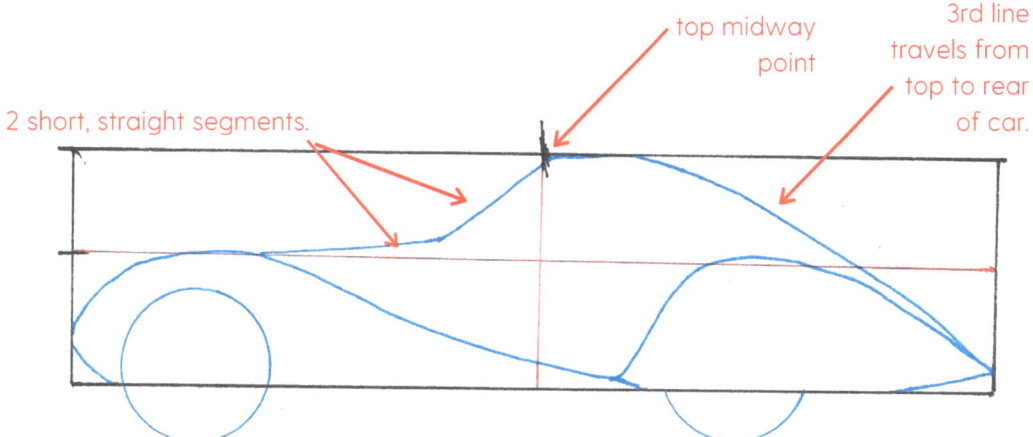

Step 2. Draw 3 more lines to create the top of the car. Two are short, straight segments and the third (that makes up the rear of the car), slopes gradually from the top midpoint, all the way to the bottom right.
Add wheels, use a template to help!

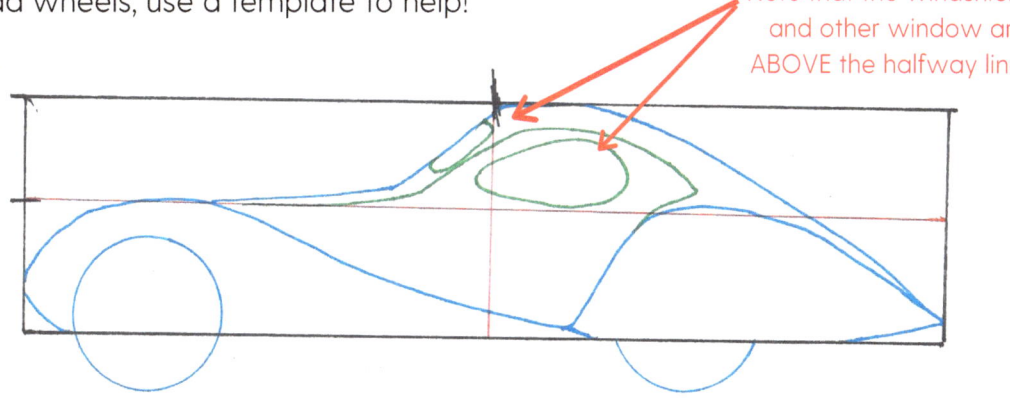

Step 3. Draw in the driver's side window and windshield. Draw the side lines for the car (all shown in green).

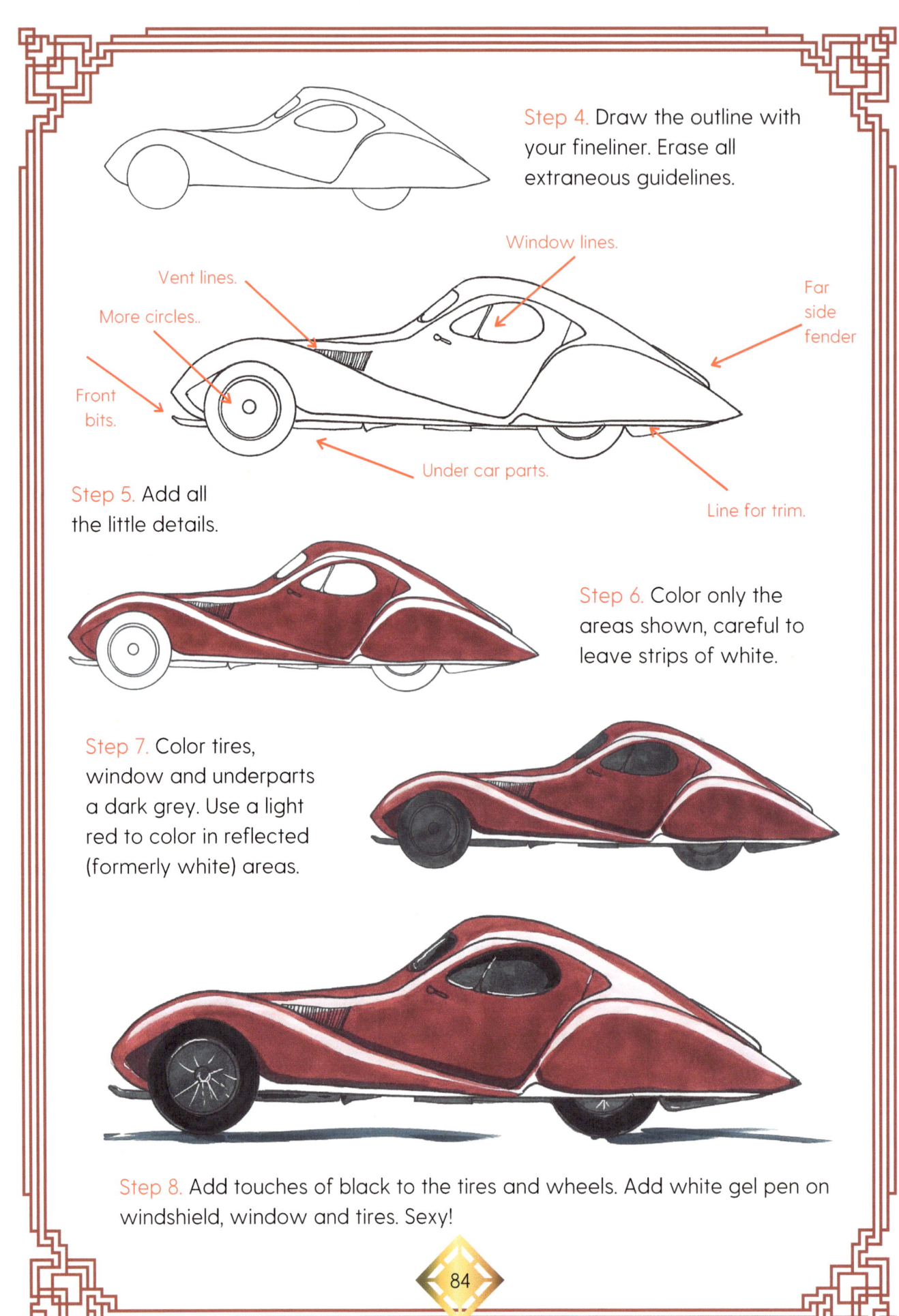

Step 4. Draw the outline with your fineliner. Erase all extraneous guidelines.

Window lines.

Vent lines.

More circles..

Front bits.

Far side fender

Under car parts.

Line for trim.

Step 5. Add all the little details.

Step 6. Color only the areas shown, careful to leave strips of white.

Step 7. Color tires, window and underparts a dark grey. Use a light red to color in reflected (formerly white) areas.

Step 8. Add touches of black to the tires and wheels. Add white gel pen on windshield, window and tires. Sexy!

1938 HISPANO-SUIZA DUBONNET XENIA (FRONT VIEW)

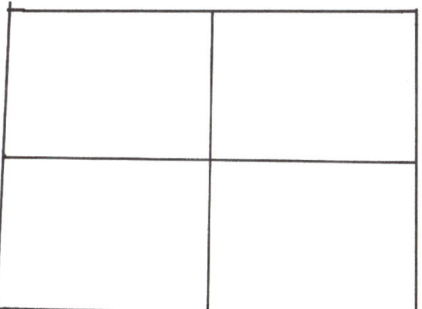

Step 1. Draw a good size rectangle and divide it into 4 **Quadrants**.

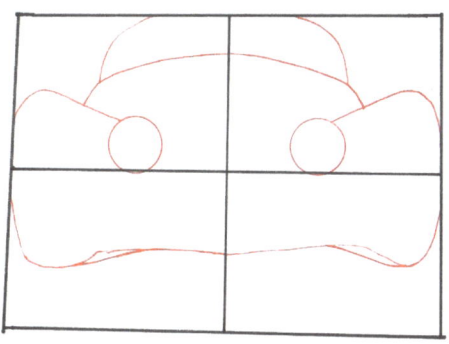

Step 2. Use the **Quadrants** to help you locate and sketch the headlights, windshield and general body shape.

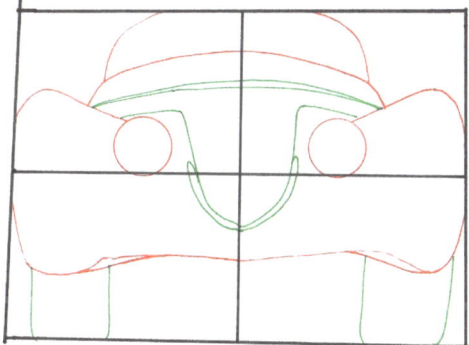

Step 3. Sketch in tires and general front hood shapes (in green). Can you see the smiley face?!

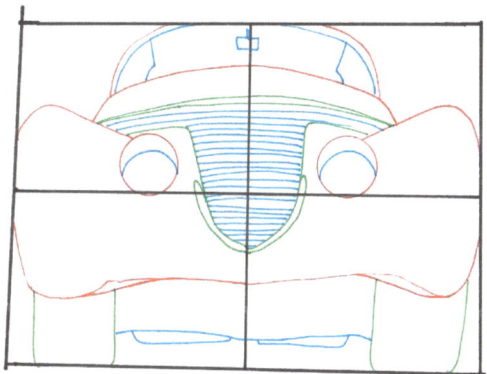

Step 4. Sketch in the details shown (in blue).

Step 5. Outline the entire car and erase your guidelines.

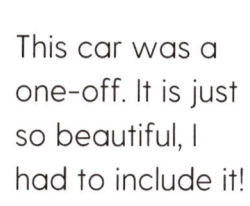

This car was a one-off. It is just so beautiful, I had to include it!

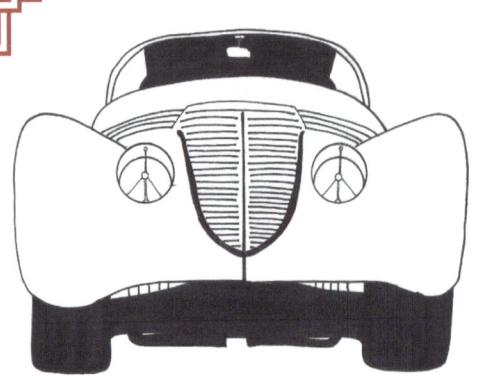
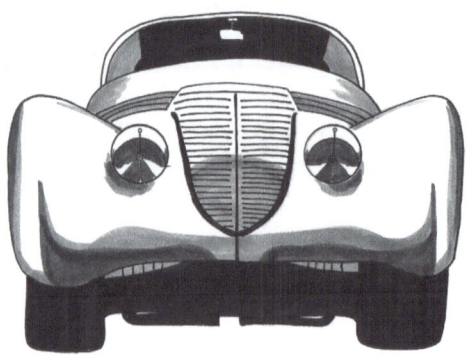

Step 6. Color the areas shown in black.

Step 7. Color the areas shown in dark grey.

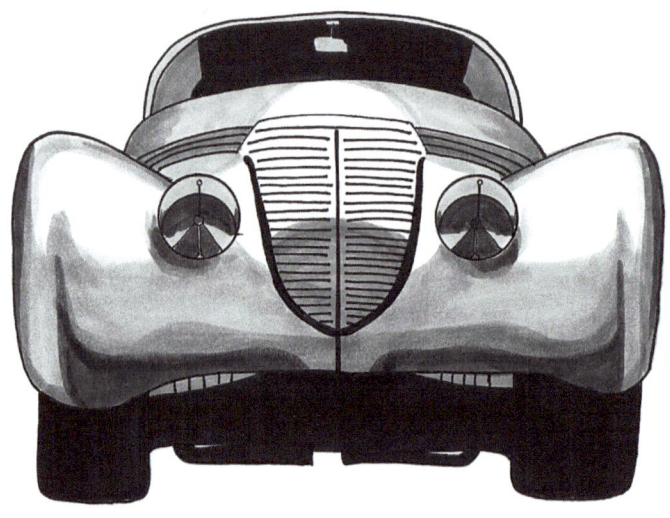

Step 8. Using a light grey this time, color a larger area, almost coloring the whole car except leaving a large area of white across the front and on the hood.

Step 9. Use a VERY light grey to go over the whole car.

Step 10. Use a white gel pen to add details on the lights.

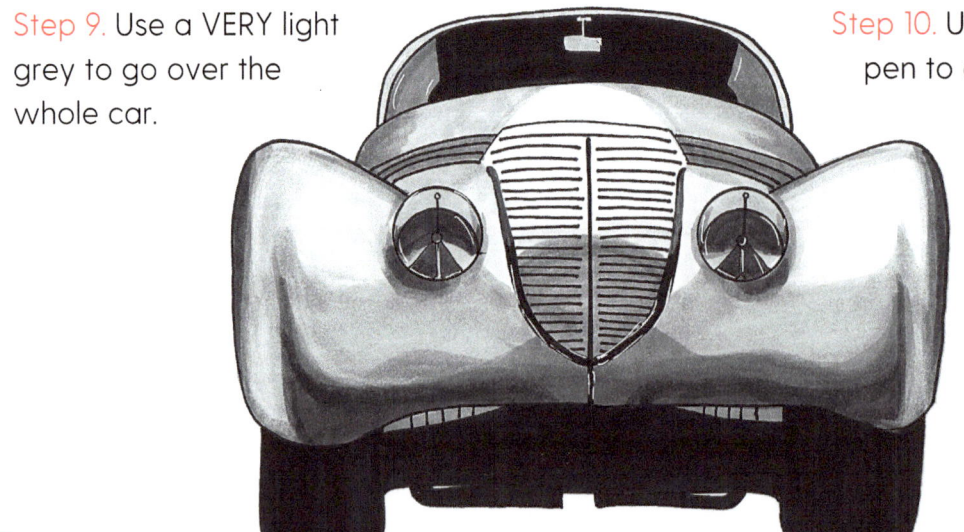

1938 HISPANO-SUIZA DUBONNET XENIA (SIDE VIEW)

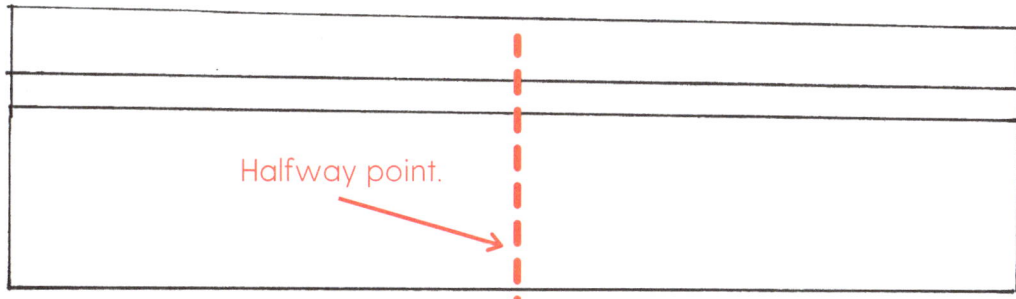

Halfway point.

Step 1. Draw a long, thin rectangle.   Then add 2 more lines on top.

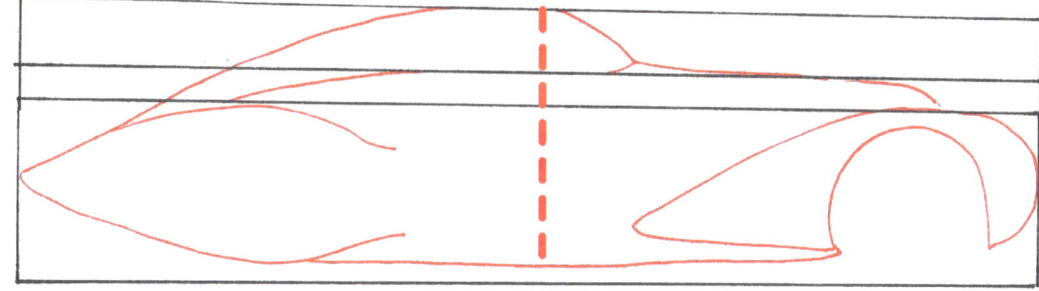

Step 2. Using the guidelines to help, sketch in the sleek lines and curves (in red).

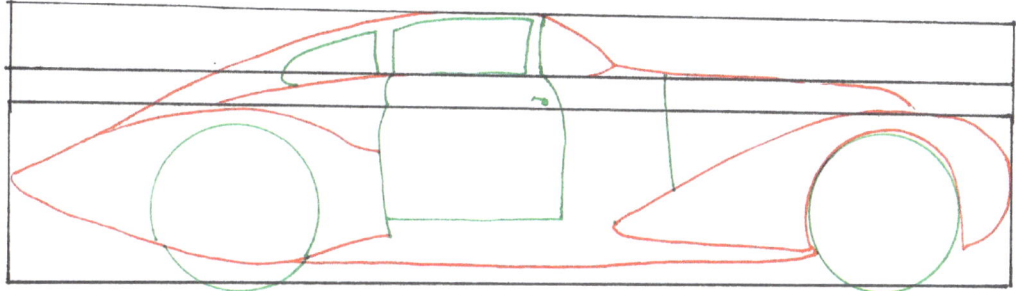

Step 3. Sketch in the tires, windows and simple door shape (in green).

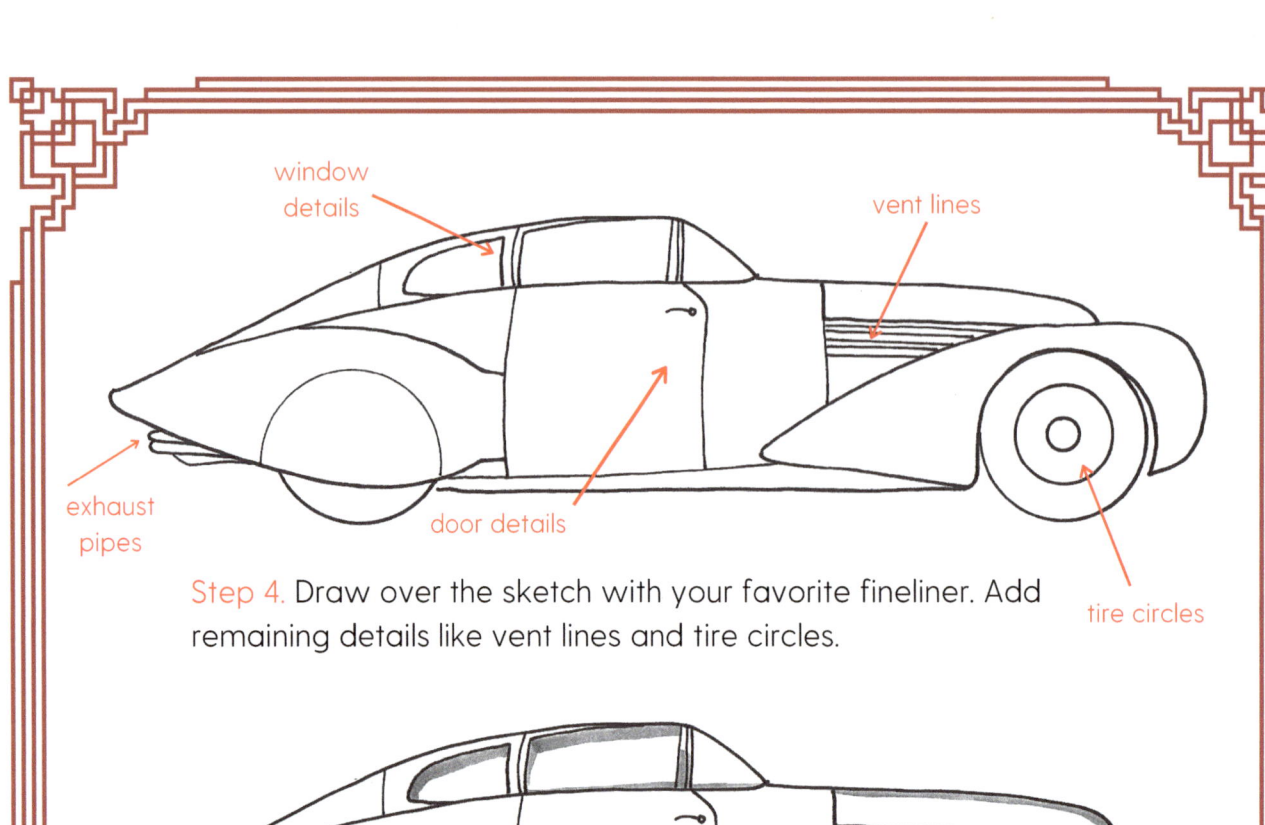

Step 4. Draw over the sketch with your favorite fineliner. Add remaining details like vent lines and tire circles.

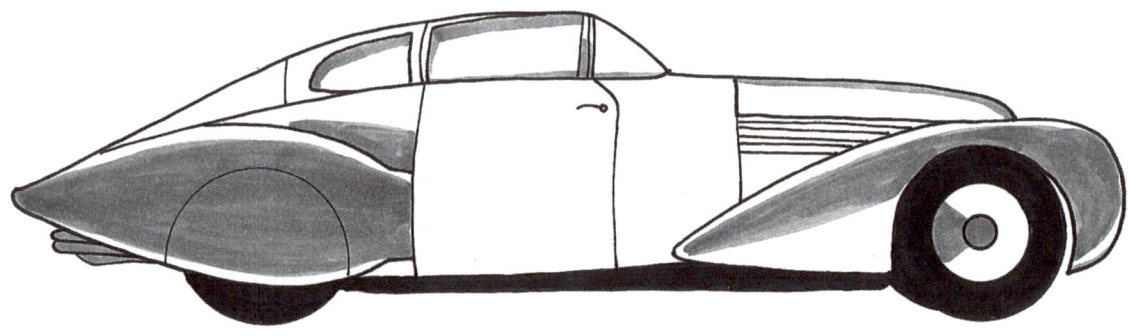

Step 5. Use black to color the underneath section and the 2 tires. Then use a mid grey tone to color just the areas shown.

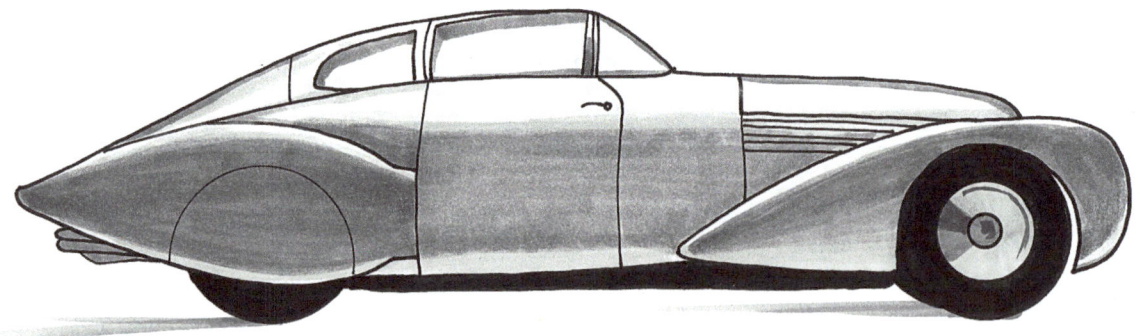

Step 6. Use lighter shades of grey to color the rest of the car. Get ready for a sweet ride!!

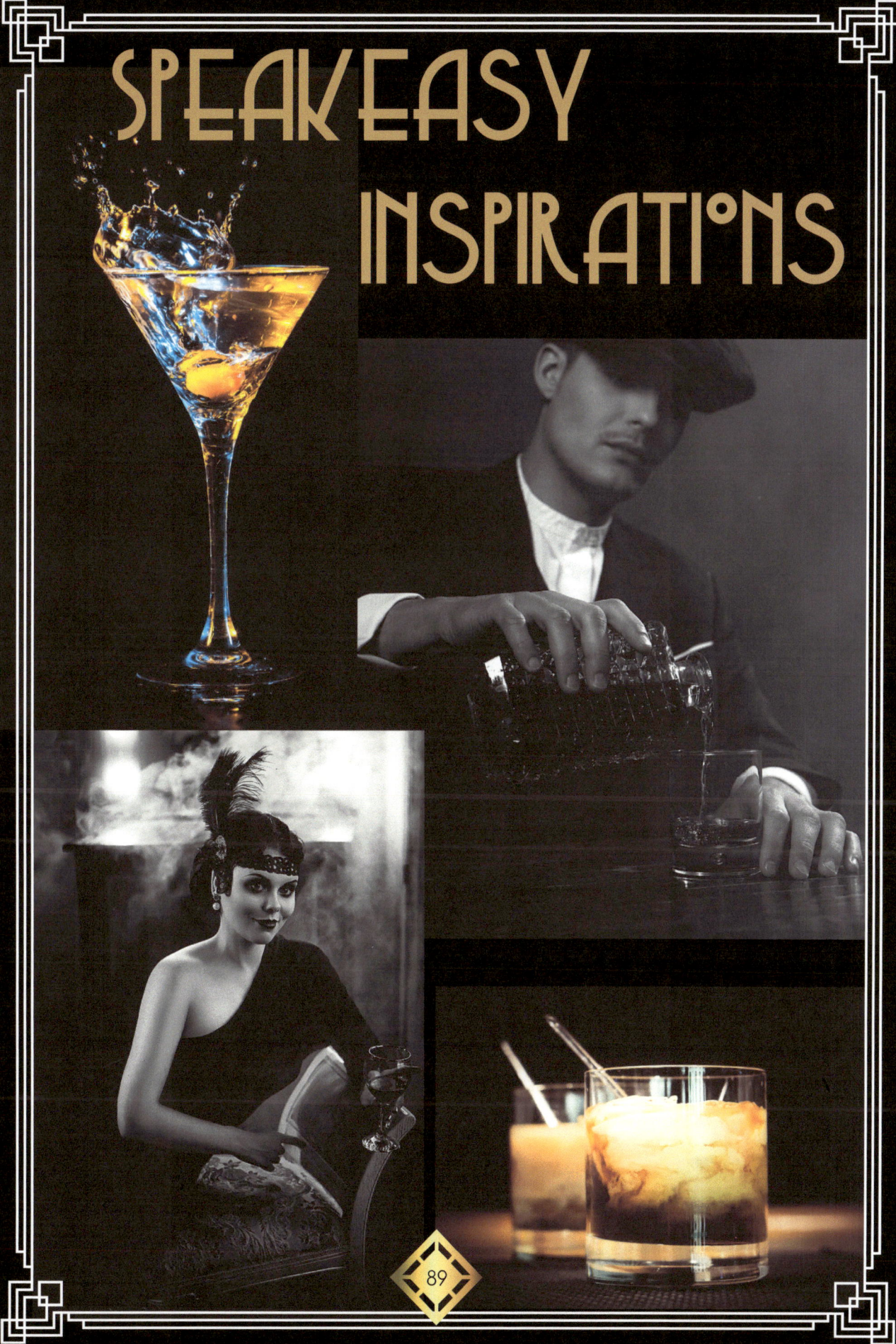

The Prohibition began in 1919 and lasted thirteen long years. While it was illegal to manufacture, sell or distribute liquor, it wasn't illegal to drink it and drink it they did! Most everyone!

This resulted in a LOT of people resorting to make their own "bootleg" variety that was foul tasting and often, downright dangerous and sometimes even fatal!

But who better to drink with than friends? Thus the "Speakeasy" was born.

One upside to the bad tasting, homemade, variety was the birth of some of the best creative cocktails of all time! These included fun and flavorful ingredients that were delicious to drink and (as it turns out) fun to draw too!

Let's raise a glass (and a pencil) to the next few pages where we will draw some of the most popular drinks of the Art Deco era.

THE COCKTAIL GLASS

Since the majority of the drinks served during this time required the use of the standard Cocktail (Martini) Glass we will learn to draw one first. Afterwards we can go through the drinks, one by one, and add the fun colors, fruits, peels and drink accessories that go with! But first things first, let's draw the glass.

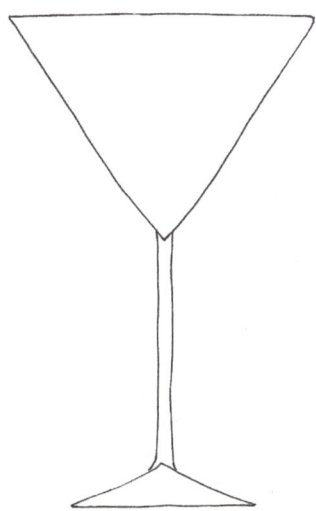

Step 1. Draw 2 triangles and 2 long parallel lines connecting them.

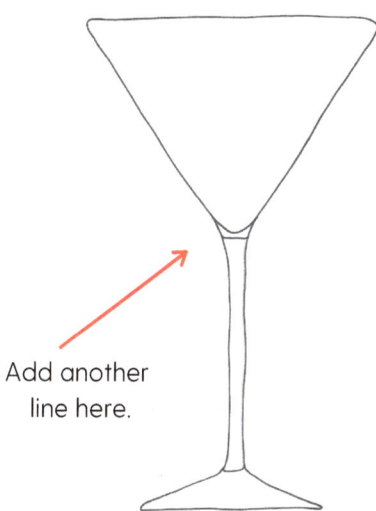

Add another line here.

Step 2. Slightly round out the edges of each triangle.

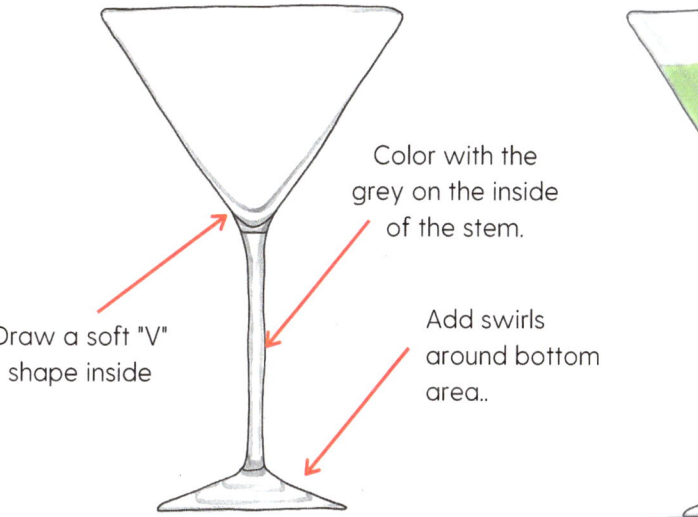

Draw a soft "V" shape inside

Color with the grey on the inside of the stem.

Add swirls around bottom area..

Step 3. Using 1 or 2 light shades of grey, draw the inside glass.

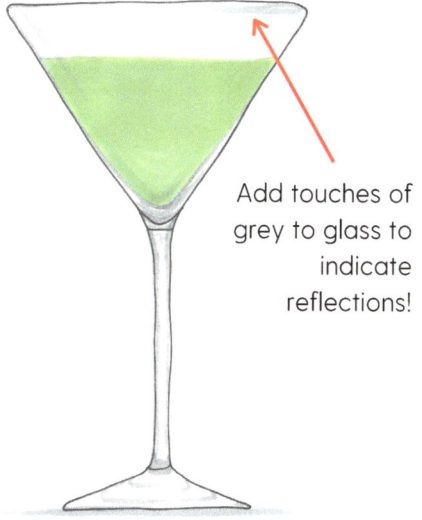

Add touches of grey to glass to indicate reflections!

Step 4. Add the liquid! Use the color of the cocktail, of course!

FALLEN ANGEL

This first glass drawing lesson segues perfectly into our very first illustrated cocktail beverage (and why let a perfectly good drink...er...drawing...go to waste?!). Bitters and creme de menthe were the perfect, strong, ingredients to help disguise the harshness of a hastily brewed bathtub gin! Plus the color green is spot on (and so fun for a drawing AND a cocktail!), so that's a bonus. All we are missing is a sprig of mint!

Step 5. (continued from previous page) Draw jagged-edged leaves coming off a short stem.

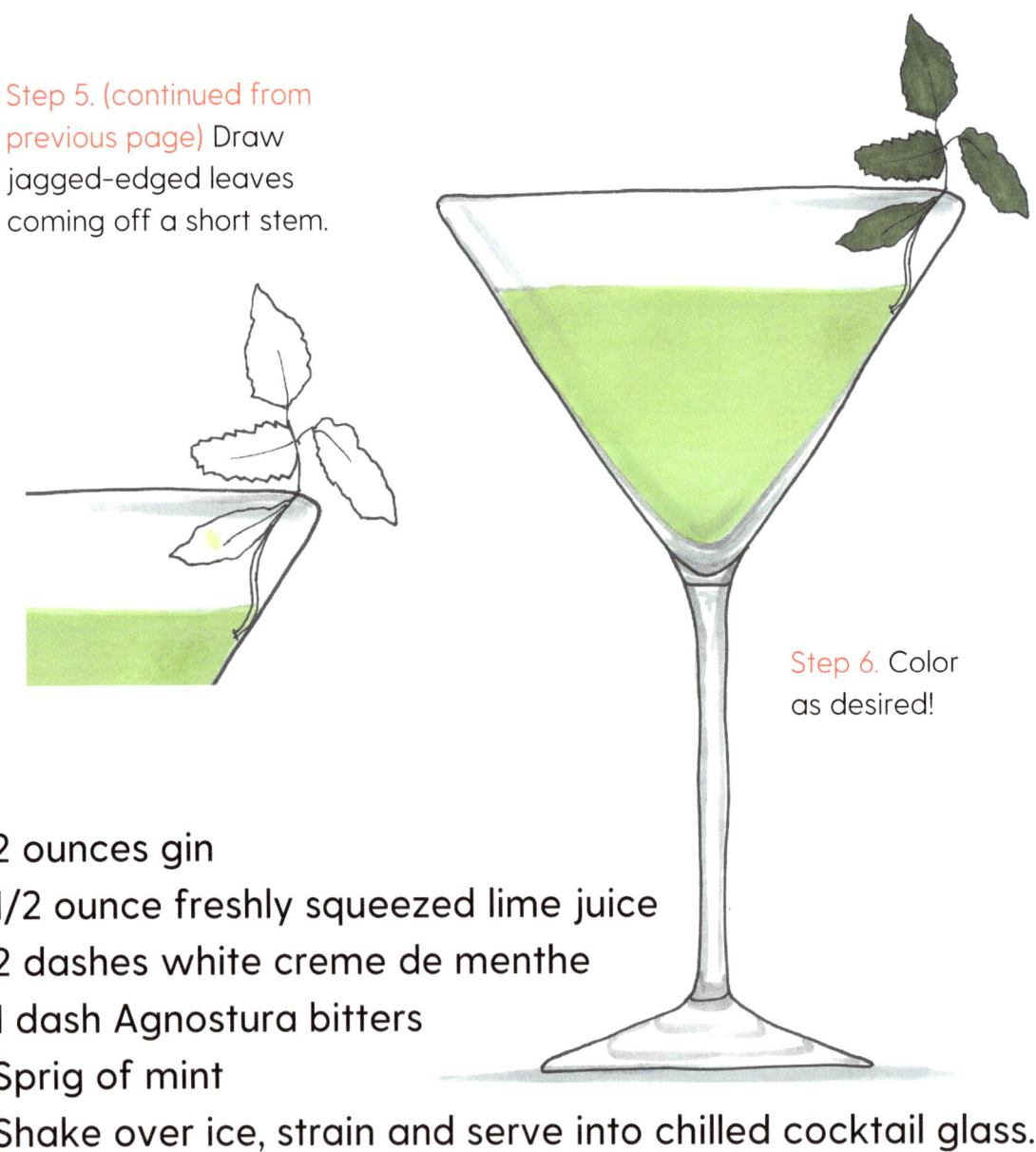

Step 6. Color as desired!

2 ounces gin
1/2 ounce freshly squeezed lime juice
2 dashes white creme de menthe
1 dash Agnostura bitters
Sprig of mint
Shake over ice, strain and serve into chilled cocktail glass.

BEES KNEES

Gin and Rum were the main staples of Prohibition which is why they are the base ingredient for most of these delicious drinks! Bees Knees means "the best" in 1920's speak and without a doubt this Gin mix has lasted the test of time for a good reason, it's delicious! The glass is the same but the lemon is new so let's learn to draw that first.

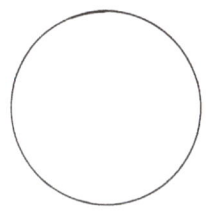
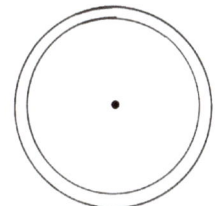
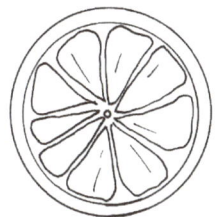

Step 1. Draw a circle (I use a template to get a good one).

Step 2. Draw a circle inside the first one. Draw a dot right in the center.

Step 3. Freehand segments around the middle point.

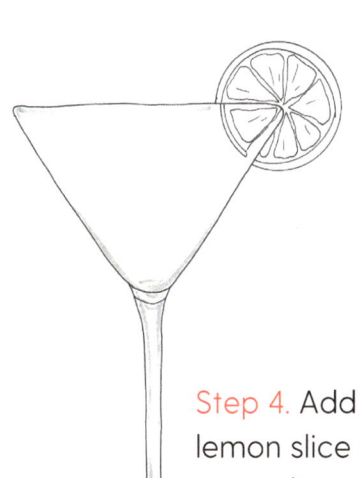
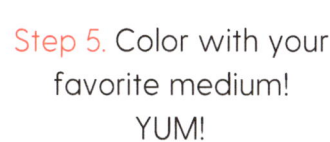

Step 4. Add the lemon slice off to one side.

Step 5. Color with your favorite medium! YUM!

The normal garnish for this drink is the lemon peel but a lemon slice is prettier I think!

2 oz gin
3/4 oz lemon juice
3/4 oz honey

Shake well over ice, strain and serve into chilled cocktail glass.

CORPSE REVIVER N°. BLUE

The Corpse Reviver Number 1 was first concocted in the late 1800's as a hangover remedy. The famous quote being that if you drink four in quick succession, you'd have enough alcohol to revive a corpse! The Number 2 rendition was very popular during the Prohibition (being Gin based), and is still popular today. Sadly, the color of that cocktail is a boring beige so for this one I thought we could draw a modern variation of the classic recipe which came about (as a joke) in 2016 but was so delicious the Corpse Reviver No. Blue has been popular and been made ever since. The best part? You guessed it.
It's BLUE.

Step 1. Let's draw a Coup glass this time (just for fun). It's the same as before, only you add a wide "U" shape instead of a "V"!

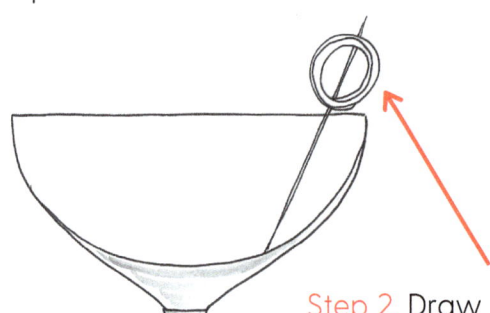

Step 2. Draw a few swirls. Then draw the toothpick through to the bottom.

3/4 oz London dry gin
3/4 oz Blue curaçao
3/4 oz Lillet Blanc
3/4 oz Lemon juice

Step 3. Fill your glass with ink or watercolor or whatever you fancy as long as it's blue!

Rinse a chilled glass with Absinthe and set aside. Shake the remaining ingredients over ice, strain and serve into chilled cocktail glass.

THE OLD FASHIONED

The original name for this classic cocktail is the "Whiskey Cocktail" and pre-dates this era by half a century. As this is served over ice, we better get to learning how to draw that! Thankfully, ice cubes are typically square and that, my friends, makes it easy.

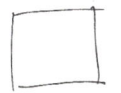 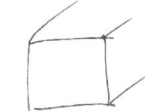 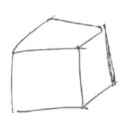 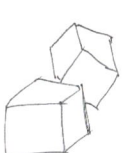 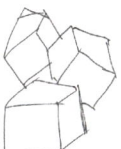

Step 1. Draw a square.

Step 2. Draw 3 lines (parallel).

Step 3. Connect those points.

Step 4. Practice stacking them up!

Don't forget the orange peel!

Add a circle and a stem for a cherry!

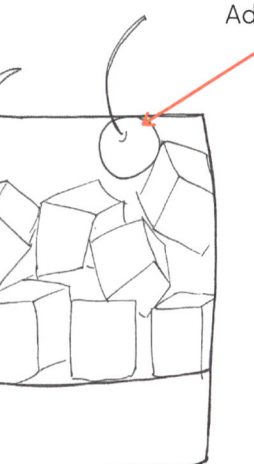

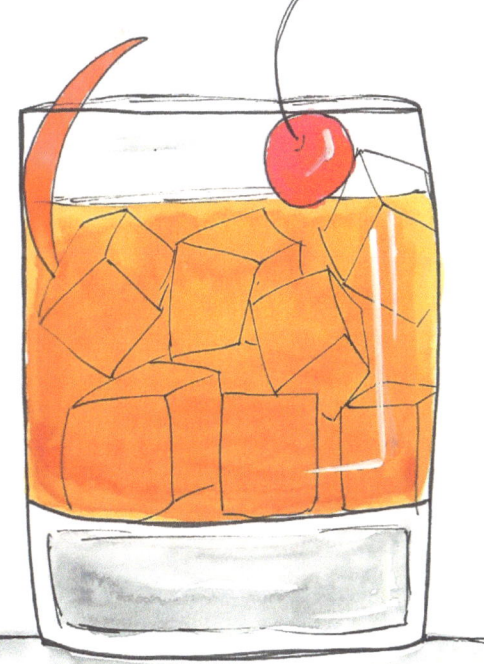

Step 4. Construct a simple rectangle shape glass with thick bottom. Stack those cubes!

1 sugar cube (or simple syrup)
2 dashes Angostura bitters
2 ounces rye or bourbon

Stir the sugar cube and bitters with one bar spoon of water at the bottom of a chilled glass. Add liquor and stir. Add ice.

FRENCH 75

Named for an intimidating gun used by the French in the first World War, this cocktail was a popular way to drown out the awful home brewed gin taste by adding a hearty dose of more booze...Champagne! And with that, we learn to draw a fancy Art Deco-style Champagne glass as well.

Step 1. Draw a elongated "U" shape. Simple stem and bottom.

Step 2. Draw 3 lines at the stem and 2 at the base.

Step 3. Add more lines as details as shown.

Step 4. Add a lemon peel swirl!

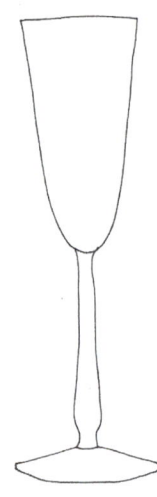
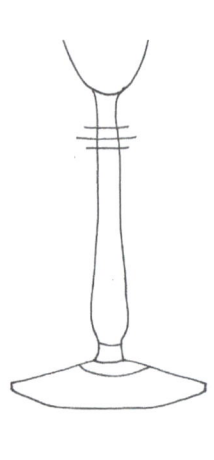
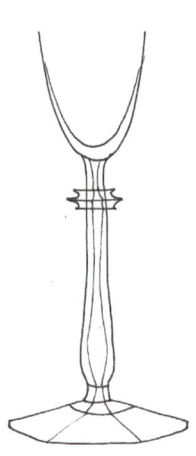
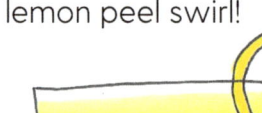

Step 5. Color your drink a pale yellow and grey for the glass. Add dots for the bubbly inside!

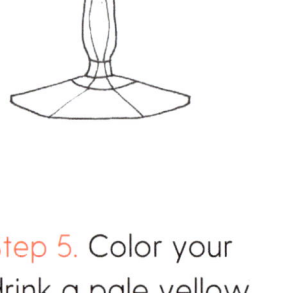

12 oz Champagne
1/2 oz Lemon juice
1 oz Gin
2 Dashes Simple syrup

Combine gin, syrup, and lemon juice in a cocktail shaker filled with ice. Shake vigorously and strain into an iced champagne glass. Top up with Champagne.

MARY PICKFORD

Named after Canadian film actress and producer, Mary Pickford, this cocktail is served shaken and chilled and is so scrumptious it's listed in the International Bartenders Association Official Cocktails guide. The drink is a vibrant orangy/red! I think this time I'm going to see what this drink looks like using my Fountain Pen inks. My bet is it's gonna be the bees knees!

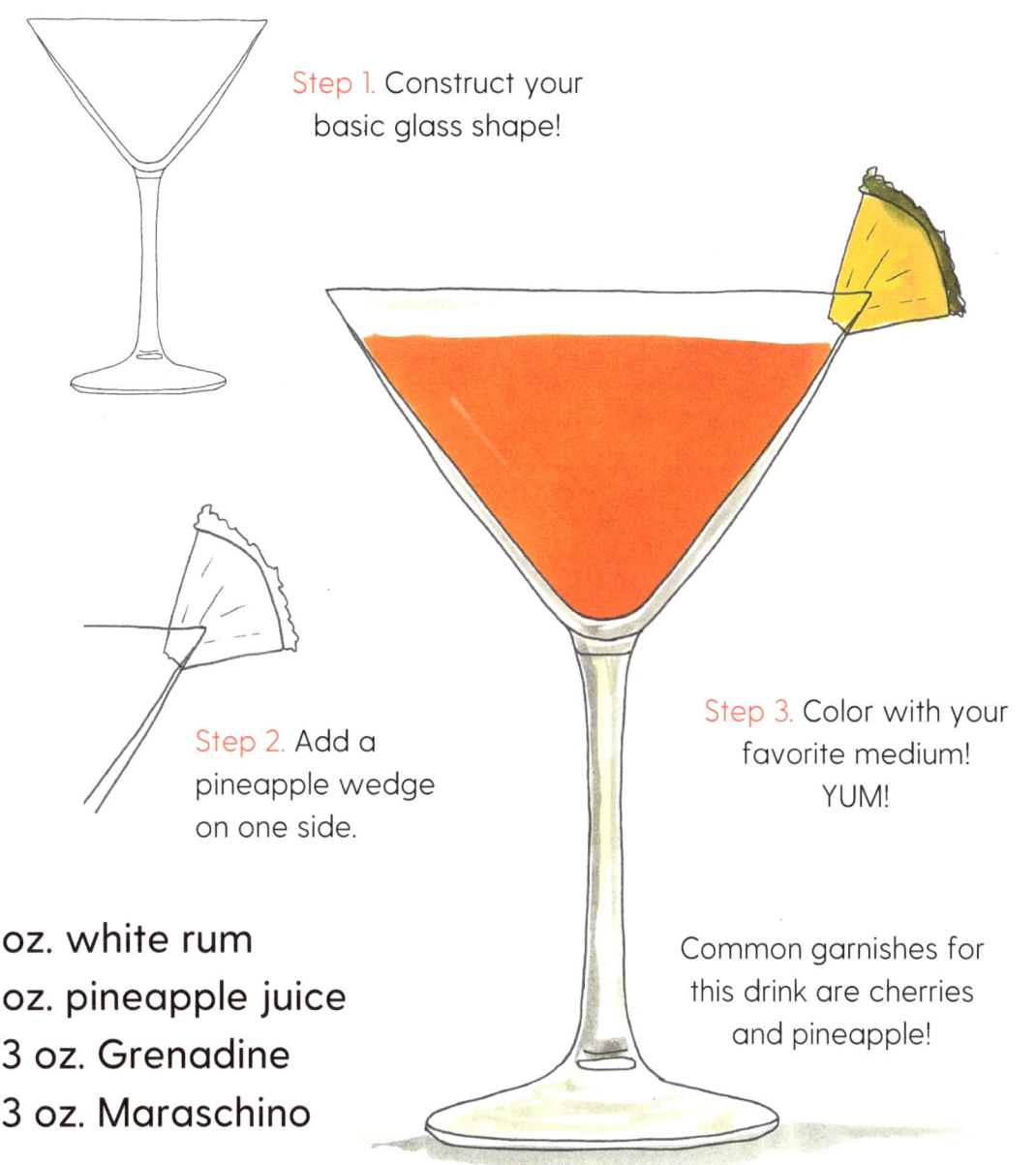

Step 1. Construct your basic glass shape!

Step 2. Add a pineapple wedge on one side.

Step 3. Color with your favorite medium! YUM!

Common garnishes for this drink are cherries and pineapple!

2 oz. white rum
2 oz. pineapple juice
1/3 oz. Grenadine
1/3 oz. Maraschino

Shake over ice, strain and serve into chilled cocktail glass.

DUBONNET

Here is yet another drink where the addition of another liquor is brought in with the sole purpose of helping the rest of the drink go down easy. In this case it's a dry French red wine but, by golly, it did the trick! It sounds fancy so I thought we could pour this one into an extra long stemmed martini glass for fun!

Step 1. Draw a super tall glass.

Step 2. Add grey to stem and base.

Step 3. Color and add lemon twist!

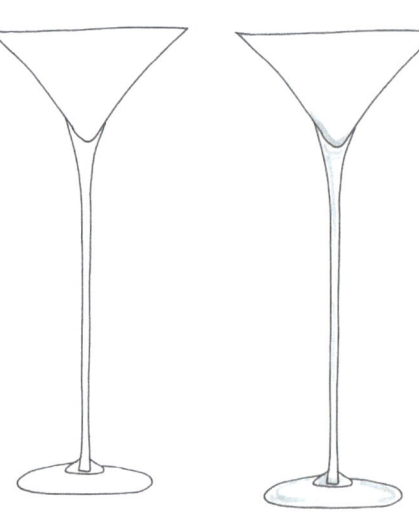

2 ounces gin
2 ounces Dubonnet (French wine)
1/2 ounce lemon juice

In a shaker with ice, add the gin, Dubonnet, and lemon juice. Shake and strain into a martini glass. Serve garnished with a twist of lemon.

SIDECAR

Unlike the other drinks listed, the Sidecar cocktail (literally named for the motorcycle sidecar), was invented during the Prohibition in 1922. Though it was dreamt up in Paris, the drink was actually created by an American. The original recipe calls for all 3 ingredients in equal parts but has evolved, overtime, to be the ratios listed here. I am presenting a small shift in the way to draw the martini glass as well, just to offer some fun differentiation!

Step 1. Draw a glass but this time, draw the line of liquid at the top.

Step 3. Freehand the citrise segments

Step 4. Color with your favorite art supply making sure to add grey to the stem!

Step 2. Use a circle template to create the orange (or lemon).

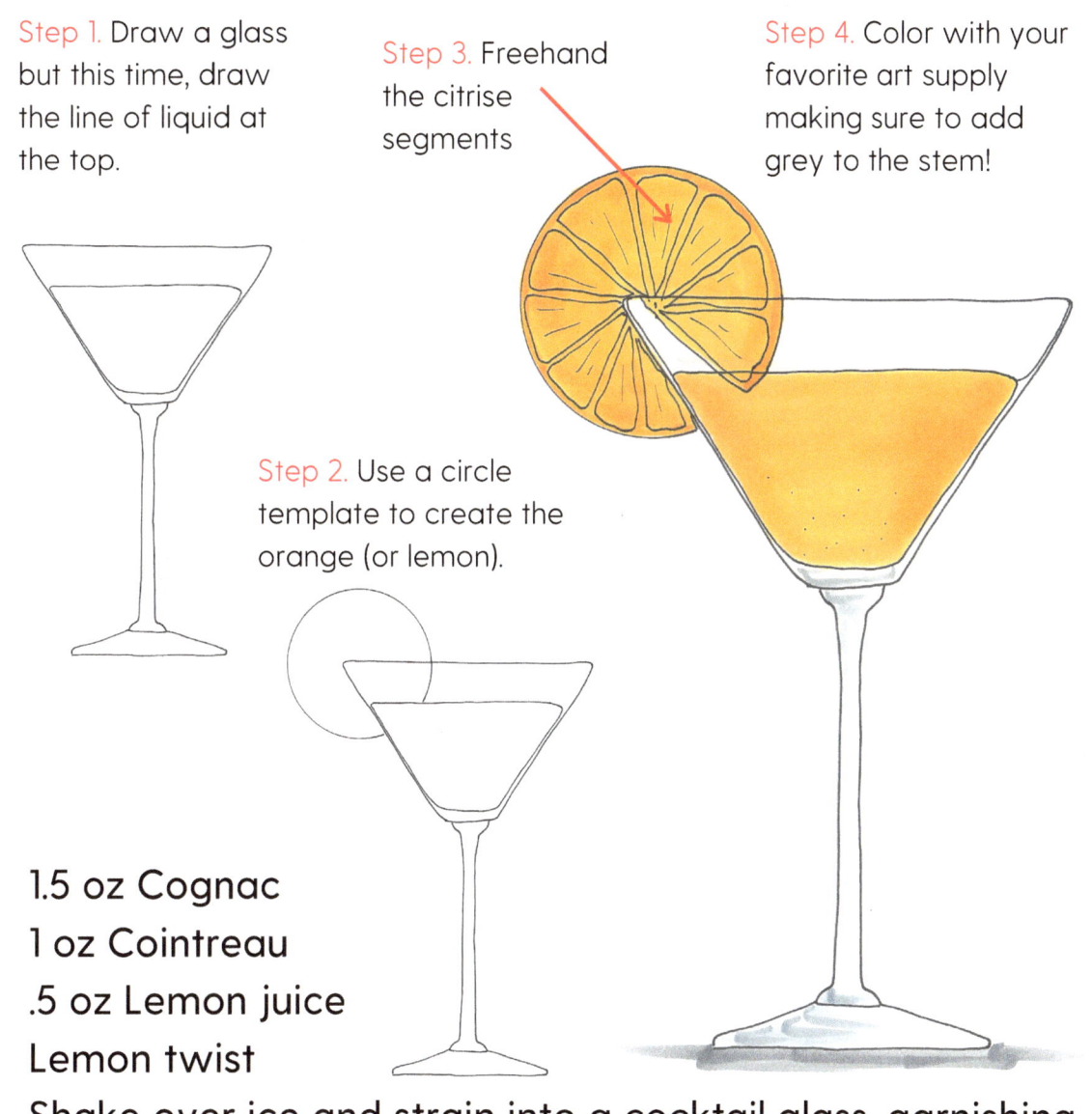

1.5 oz Cognac
1 oz Cointreau
.5 oz Lemon juice
Lemon twist

Shake over ice and strain into a cocktail glass, garnishing with the twist (shown above with orange slice).

WARD 8

Although the name originated with honor (in recognition of a powerful Massachusetts politician winning his seat in 1898) the reason the drink became so popular during the Prohibition was that it straight-up made the taste of shady or dubious rye whiskey palatable! The hearty doses of grenadine and juices masked foul tastes well and stretched the rye supply to boot! Just for fun we will draw it in a stemless martini glass this time.

Step 1. Draw a rounded "v" shape and a rounded base.

Step 2. Draw a soft "v" inside the first one. Add grey to outside and base.

Step 3. Add 2 cherries!

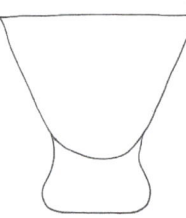
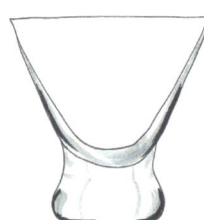
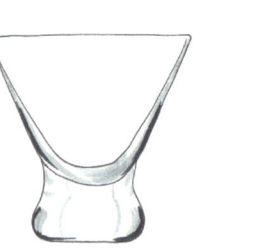

Step 4. Color with your favorite medium! Add white highlights to cherries and drink. Enjoy!

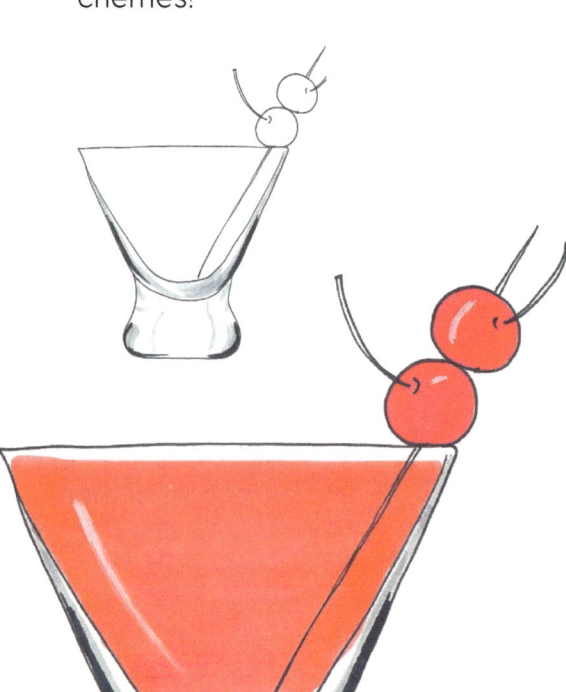

2 ounces rye whiskey
1/2 ounce lemon juice
1/2 ounce orange juice
1 teaspoon grenadine
Maraschino cherry (optional)

In a shaker, combine the whiskey, lemon juice, orange juice, and grenadine with ice. Strain into a chilled glass.

Now let your imagination and drawing fun truly begin!

Wouldn't it be fun to imagine how the characters from Vol. 1 would interact with some of the drawings we've done from Vol. 2?

A night on the town? Perhaps?

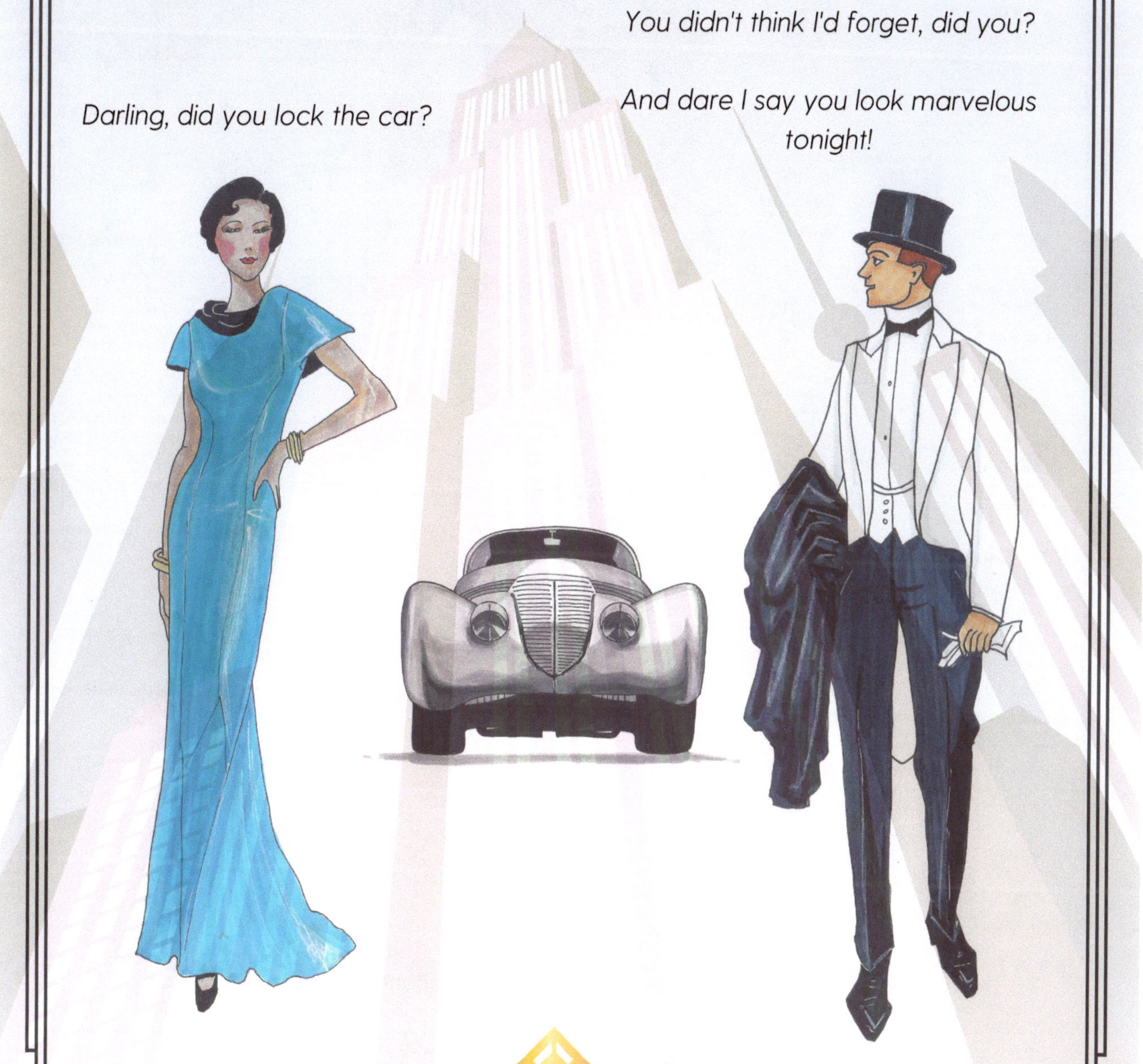

Darling, did you lock the car?

You didn't think I'd forget, did you?

And dare I say you look marvelous tonight!

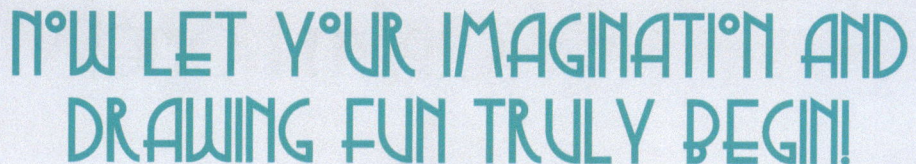

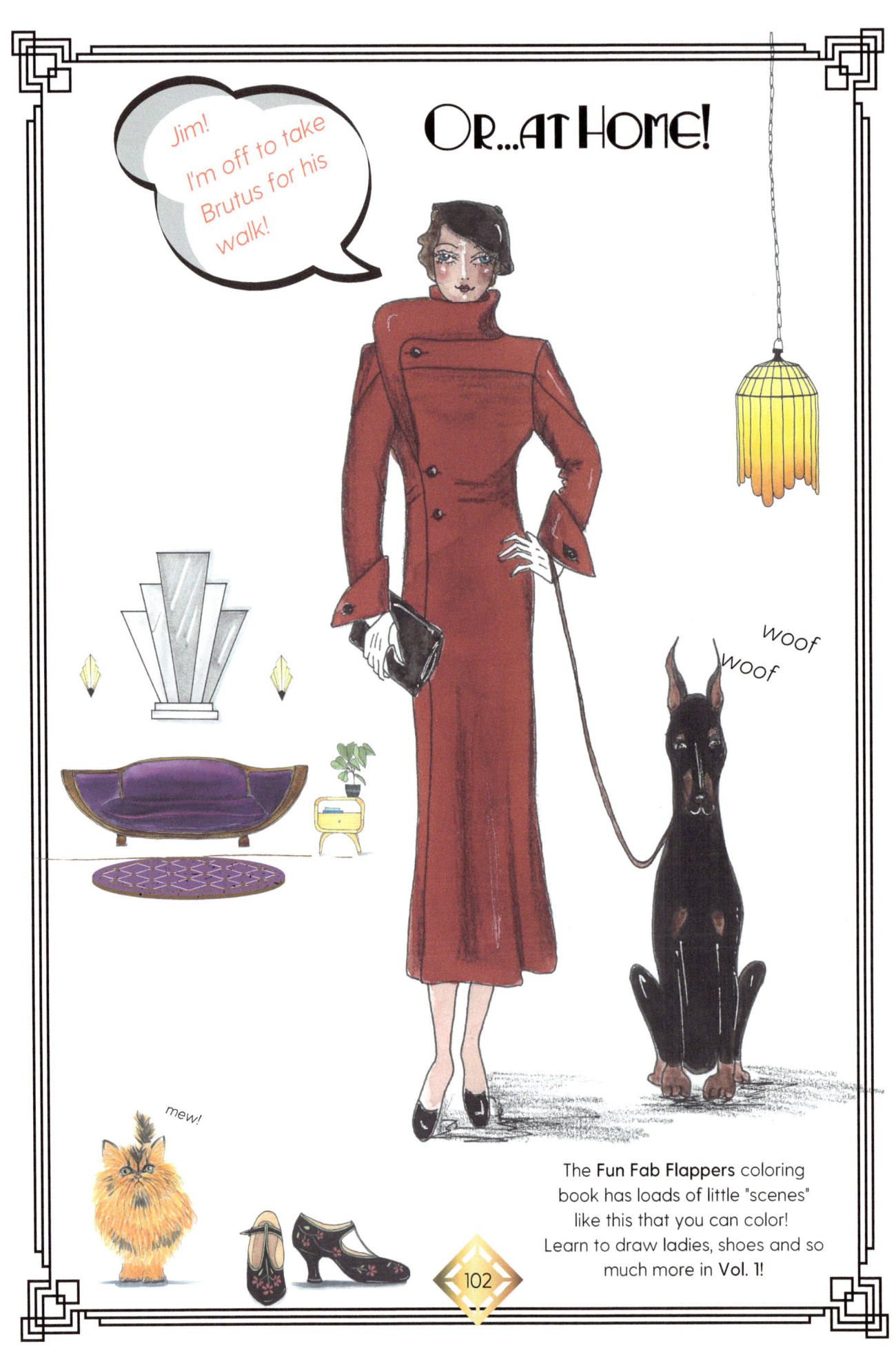

ABOUT THE AUTHOR

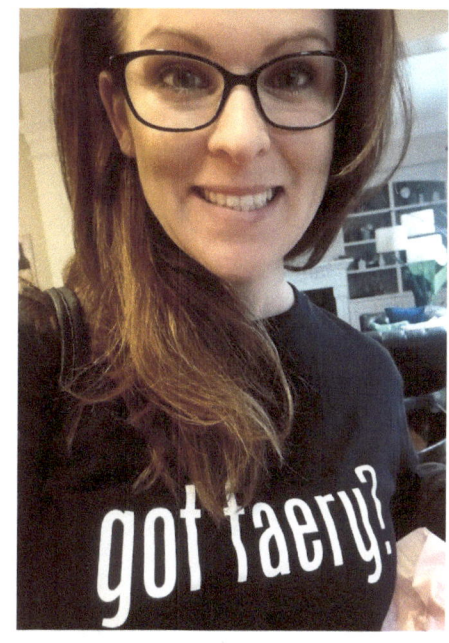

Karen Campbell is a Boston area native who lives in North Carolina with her husband, three boy humans and three girl cats. She is a full time artist, instructor, business owner and is the author of many fun drawing and mixed media art books.

She started teaching art in 2011 and founded her online art school, Awesome Art School, in 2016. Thanks to her school and 2 art-based YouTube Channels, Karen has had the pleasure of impacting the lives of tens of thousands of adult learners across the globe with fun art lessons.

Karen's primary goal is to make art easy and accessible to everyone. Besides techniques, she focuses her students attention on becoming better artists through the practice of having pure, unadulterated FUN!!! Subscribe to her YouTube channel for your own weekly dose! http://bit.ly/karendraws

MORE ART DECO

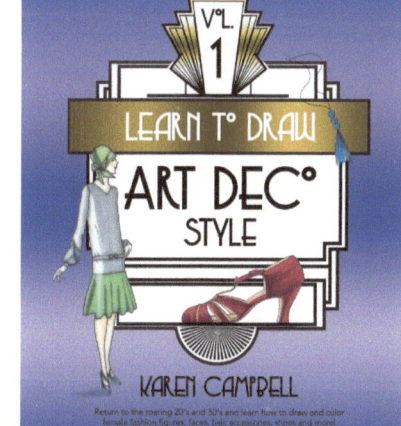

The first installment of Art Deco awesomeness! Chalk full of fun fabulous figures, flappers, fashion, jewelry, shoes and more!

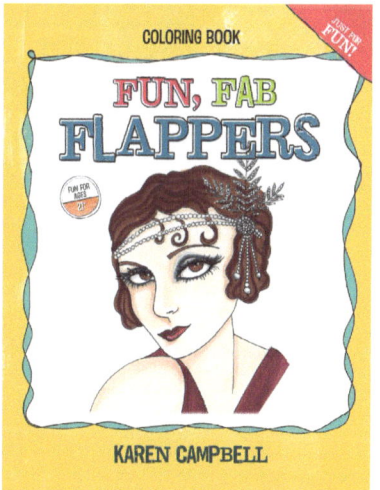

Hundreds of large graphic Art Deco illustrations and designs for endless hours of coloring FUN! Come play!

MORE BOOKS BY KAREN CAMPBELL

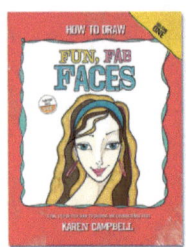 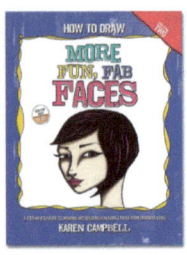 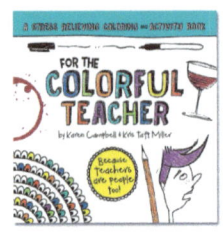

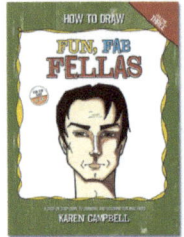 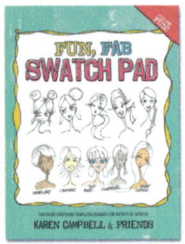 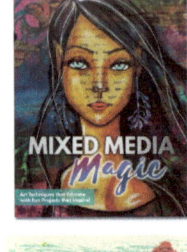

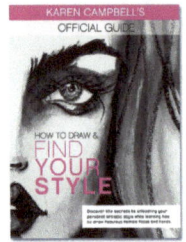 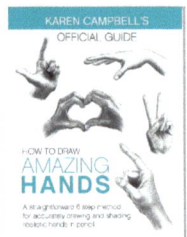 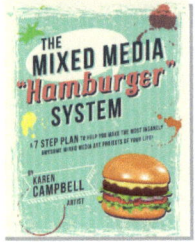

 awesomeartschool.com

 karencampbellartist.com

 bit.ly/karendraws (youtube drawing channel)

 youtube.com/karencampbellartist (mixed media)

 facebook.com/karencampbellartist

 instagram.com/karencampbellartist

 pinterest.com/karencampbellartist

 amazon.com/author/karencampbell

 etsy.com/shop/karencampbellartist

 patreon.com/karencampbellartist

www.ingramcontent.com/pod-product-compliance
Lightning Source LLC
Chambersburg PA
CBHW051153220526
45473CB00003B/763